The Impact of Classroom Practices

A volume in
Contemporary Perspectives on Access, Equity, and Achievement
Chance W. Lewis, *Series Editor*

The Impact of Classroom Practices

Teacher Educators' Reflections on Culturally Relevant Teachers

edited by

Antonio L. Ellis
American University

Nathaniel Bryan
Miami University

Yolanda Sealey-Ruiz
Teachers College, Columbia University

Ivory Toldson
Howard University

Christopher Emdin
Teachers College, Columbia University

INFORMATION AGE PUBLISHING, INC.
Charlotte, NC • www.infoagepub.com

Library of Congress Cataloging-in-Publication Data

A CIP record for this book is available from the Library of Congress
http://www.loc.gov

ISBN: 978-1-64802-398-9 (Paperback)
978-1-64802-399-6 (Hardcover)
978-1-64802-400-9 (E-Book)

Printed in the United States of America

*This book is dedicated to Mr. Linard H. McCloud,
who is the longest employed teacher at Burke High School in Charleston,
South Carolina. We celebrate his 40 years of effective teaching at the same school.
To honor his commitment to education, we share our reflections
on effective teaching through critical storytelling.*

CONTENTS

FOREWORD

William F. Tate IV

I love biographical stories. Throughout my professional career, I have enjoyed reading résumés, CVs, bio statements, and other documents that provide insight into the lives of my colleagues and associates. I aspire to understand better the relationship between their accomplishments and the various forms of sponsored mobility in their lives. How did the individuals learn to navigate their situation? Who helped them move to the next phase in their lives?

My fascination with stories about life-course started early. *Biography* the American documentary television series was a staple during my youth. As a child, I loved the reruns of the show *This is Your Life.* The origin of the show dates to 1940s radio. The television show experienced fits of starts and stops on the airways from the 1950s to earlier 2000s. One of my favorite episodes highlighted the life of Muhammad Ali. Most of the episodes followed a formula. And the Ali episode was no different. The star of the hour arrives at the television set thinking he is headed to an important engagement unrelated to the story of his life. Shocked when he arrives at the set, Mr. Ali professes his love for the show and can't believe his life will be shared for all to see.

As you might imagine, the Muhammad Ali episode evolved with a series of guests arriving to share their part in his life. His wife, parents, children, professional trainer, amateur and professional boxing opponents, friends,

The Impact of Classroom Practices, pages ix–xi

fellow Olympians, and youth sports leaders paraded onto the set to offer perspective and tales. There were two major takeaways from this episode. The first take away entailed Muhammad Ali's desperate attempt to interject his views. He wanted us to hear how he interpreted the story. Time and the show's protocol prohibited his contribution. A second take away involved one of the guests. She provided tremendous insight into the boxer's life. And of all the guests, she is the one person that offered a perspective on the champion from both his youth and his adult life. Mrs. Carter, his third-grade teacher, bridged the seasons of his life. She described his temperament as a child. And Mrs. Carter offered a view into the logic underpinning her instruction to the 8-year old version of arguably the greatest boxer of all time. Specifically, she discouraged him from street fighting. She told him that fighting would not take him far. Ali's look of respect and admiration for his former teacher was apparent. Mrs. Carter continued by discussing her career transition to head the YWCA. She sent for her former student to make a speech at a YWCA event and he had obliged. Mrs. Carter added that the boxer wrote a check for $10,000 on the spot to help the kids in the YWCA program. It is here that the multigenerational effects of the student–teacher relationship emerge. The teacher who sponsored a young Ali's mobility reaches out to him to give back to his community. And he responded. Mrs. Carter's words illustrate the importance of this multigenerational transaction.

This volume provides the field a retrospective view of a group of "Mrs. Carters" who impacted the lives of educators and scholars. Unlike the protocol of *This is Your Life,* the authors narrate the story and shape our understanding of how teachers influenced their life-course, worldviews, and approaches to education. We hear their voices reflecting on childhood and the adolescent years, enabling us to grow in our understanding of the multigenerational nature of the student–teacher relationship. Specifically, we learn more about how a group of intellectuals interpret past engagement with impactful educators and the influence of these interactions on their practices, thinking, and scholarly outlook.

Years ago, I argued that my schoolboy experiences in urban schools with great teachers represented important lessons for the field. However, custom and tradition prohibited these experiences from inclusion in the literature. Specifically, the paradigmatic boundaries of my field of study aligned with the documentary series, *This is Your Life.* It was acceptable to interview others about my experiences and to synthesize their views as a form of evidence. However, crossing the standing protocol of excluding my story and my interpretation of events posed a threat to the validity and trustworthiness of the information. I countered with the need to examine the lives of rare birds in the academy. In the case of this book, I invite the readers to examine each chapter and to glean lessons from the experiences of my colleagues. They have navigated the scholarly road to the highest levels of graduate education attainment. This is their life.

CHAPTER 1

MR. LINARD H. McCLOUD

Clarifying Excellence in Teacher Education Practice

Antonio L. Ellis

For over three decades educational researchers and scholars have largely written about teacher effectiveness using quantitative research methodologies (Darling-Hammond, Holtzman, Gatlin, & Heilig, 2005; Ingersoll & Strong, 2011; Wilson & Hallum, 2006). There is a dearth of literature available that defines teacher effectiveness using the reflective voices of former students (Ladson-Billings, 1995; Siddle Walker, 2001, 2005). Debates regarding the qualities, skills, and dispositions of effective teachers and teaching have raged in teacher education for several decades. Ladson-Billings' (2009) *The Dreamkeepers: Successful Teachers of African American Children* was a pathbreaking work that has become a foundational study that informs the work of culturally relevant (Ladson-Billings, 2009) and "culturally sustaining" (Paris & Alim, 2017) teaching. In her book *The Dreamkeepers,* Ladson-Billings describes effective teachers who are able to draw from the cultural wealth of Black communities. These Dreamkeepers ensured that their Black students were academically successful and grew both in terms of their

The Impact of Classroom Practices, pages 1–6

cultural competence and their sociopolitical awareness. In other words, according to Ladson-Billings (2009), these effective teachers possessed both pedagogical and relational dispositions, which leave lifelong impacts on the academic and social lives of their students. As some scholars have noted, what remains missing from the research on culturally-relevant and even culturally-sustaining teachers are "narratives" (read: stories, cuentos, testimonios, etc.) related to how the race of particular K–12 teachers positively impact the lives of their students because they either served as windows or mirrors (Bryan, 2020; Howard, 2001; Irvine & Fenwick, 2011; Milner, 2011). This volume aims to help fill this gap in educational research literature.

The foundation of this volume stems from the classroom experiences provided to me by my high school music teacher. In August of 1995, I entered Burke High School in Charleston, South Carolina; as an urban student who was placed in speech therapy, special education, and lower tracked courses (Ellis & Hartlep, 2017). I lacked motivation towards education and the majority of my teachers did not have high expectations of me. Members of my family averaged an 8th grade education. While growing up, I was encouraged to do enough just to get by academically and in life. From my recollection, all of my family members who raised me did not complete high school. Some dropped out prior to high school. Based on my surroundings and the odds that were against me, my chances for success appeared to be extremely dismal. Many people in society gave up on me, including school teachers, guidance counselors, clergy, and community leaders. Eventually I felt like all hope was lost and never imagined that I would graduate from high school.

Upon entering Burke High School, I decided to seek membership into the marching band. At that time I knew very little about musical instruments. I simply thought that joining the band program would be a fun thing to do. As I reflect on the first band practice of that school year, I recall the music teacher and marching band director, Mr. Linard McCloud's "pep talk." Everyone was completely silent as he talked in a very low and firm tone, explaining his expectation of all band members. He was very clear about what he expected from all students. Not only did he express his expectations of band students, he also talked about his expectations for the alumni of the band program. That was the first time I heard the term "alumni." Later I learned that "alumni" meant students who had graduated.

Mr. McCloud showcased the success of alumni who once were members of the marching band. In some cases, he invited alumni to speak during band practices. In other instances, it was normal for alumni to randomly stop by to visit Mr. McCloud and encourage students. During those times, Mr. McCloud typically introduced them by telling band members when they graduated and what they did post high school graduation. Unbeknownst to my peers and I, being exposed to successful alumni was another method our music teacher used to model his high expectations of us. I recall meeting marching band alumni from various fields including education, art and entertainment, medical science, carpentry, law, theology, political science, electrical engineering, auto mechanics, just to name a few.

In addition to professional fields, I remember meeting alumni who joined the United States military. Subconsciously constantly being exposed to generations of successful people who once were students inspired me to aim for success so that I could one day return to inspire students. When former students visited, I observed the proud look on Mr. McCloud's face and the spark in his eyes, as if they were his own children. In those moments, I became determined to make him equally as proud after I graduated.

Mr. McCloud made it clear that he expected all his students to achieve at least a 3.0 grade point average. In addition, he made it known that students would not be allowed to participate in the band if they consistently failed academically. In order to ensure that students succeeded, he hosted study groups at the band room an hour before school began, during lunch, and up to 3 hours after school. Due to Mr. McCloud's track record for producing highly successful students, he was highly revered in the community and among families. Therefore, if he recommended that students come to school an hour earlier and stay later for academic assistance, parents complied. In many cases parents and legal guardians were also alumni who viewed the music teacher as a father figure. Broughton (this volume) highlights the importance of educators building relationships with students and their families, just as Mr. McCloud championed.

In addition to Mr. McCloud's relationship with his students and their families, he also established strong partnerships with local businesses, which provided internships and paid work-based learning opportunities for students. Those partnerships helped fund band trips to colleges and universities and new uniforms. Local partnerships were vital because several students, including myself, could not afford to pay for these trips without additional financial support. Because Mr. McCloud believed in fostering independence and a strong work ethic in his students. He'd ensure that at least 50% of the trip was paid for, while he created opportunities for students to raise the remaining balance with structured fundraisers such as fruit drives, candy sales, soul food dinners, and bake sales. In retrospect, I understand that he supported his students while also ensuring that we earned everything we received. In order to ensure that students' needs were met, Mr. McCloud was one of the first persons who arrived at school daily and among the last to leave. Out of my 4 years in high school, I do not remember him being absent no more than once or twice. I do not highlight his attendance record to suggest that teachers should not take off as needed. Self-care and mental breaks are important for teachers. However,

I highlight Mr. McCloud's attendance record to show the depth of his commitment to his students.

Mr. McCloud was the first adult in my life who influenced me to aim high academically. He refused to settle for less from any of his students' regardless if they were in special education, general education courses, or the gifted and talented program. His level of expectation remained consistent for all of us. As a result of his demand for excellence, I eventually started rising to his expectation. By the time I became a sophomore, my respect for Mr. McCloud climaxed and I loved being a member of the band. Thereafter, I worked hard academically so that I would not disappoint the band director, who was also my music teacher. Before I knew it, I was a junior and finally a graduating senior. Mr. McCloud ensured that all seniors auditioned for music scholarships at several universities. To my surprise, I received full music scholarships to Benedict College, Florida Agricultural and Mechanical University, and South Carolina State University. Shortly after receiving the music scholarships, I became the first person from my family to graduate from high school and enter college.

While in college, I often reflected on Mr. McCloud's expectation of alumni. He always said, "We send you to college to graduate." Therefore, in the back of my mind I always told myself, "I better do well in college because I cannot return home to Mr. McCloud without a degree." By that time, I had started to believe in myself as a young adult and engaged in self-empowering activities such as reading extensively, building relationships with progressive people, and pursued memberships into organizations on campus such as Alpha Phi Alpha fraternity and the gospel choir. Eventually, I became interested in furthering my education through graduate school. Upon completing my undergraduate degree in philosophy, I entered graduate school programs at Howard University and The George Washington University, earning three master's degrees consecutively, followed by a doctoral degree in educational leadership and policy studies.

It is because of the culturally responsive and effective teaching that Mr. McCloud delivered in the classroom and beyond, that I went from being a special education student at a Title I school to possessing a doctoral degree. His pedagogical practices directly aligned with Ladson-Billings (1995) culturally relevant pedagogy tenets, which includes academic success, cultural competence, and critical consciousness. I encourage all pre-service and in-service teachers, educational leaders, and policy makers to use Mr. Linard McCloud as a model for educating children. As a current school administrator, I frequently tell stories about Mr. McCloud to my teachers, particularly to improve our family engagement, classroom management, teaching practices, and student–teacher relationships. Similarly, as a university professor who develops future teachers and school administrators,

I consistently present Mr. McCloud as a model of excellence for culturally responsive and relevant teaching.

RECOMMENDATIONS FOR TEACHER EDUCATION PRACTITIONERS

Each chapter in this volume will share similar stories about teachers whom the authors deem as effective, while concluding with practical recommendations for current and pre-service teachers to employ in their practices. Likewise, I share my practical recommendations for teachers and those who are studying to become teachers based on my experience with Mr. McCloud, whom I consider to be a Dreamkeeper. I recommend teachers employ the following practices that do not require hierarchical permission or district funding, but do require intentional planning, intrinsic motivation, and a strong work ethic:

- Be clear about your expectations and build capacity for students to meet them.
- Be fully present for your students (i.e., physically, emotionally, and mentally).
- Show students various forms of successful outcomes (i.e., alumni and mentors).
- Build relationships with families and partnerships with community stakeholders.
- Be culturally relevant and culturally responsive inside the classroom and beyond.
- Support students while also teaching them self-sufficiency and independency.
- Provide opportunities for your students beyond the classroom setting (i.e., fieldtrips, internships, and workforce development).
- Be consistent.

REFERENCES

Bryan, N. (2020, April 28). "To me, he teaches like the child learns:" Black maternal caregivers on the pedagogies and schooling practices of a Black male kindergarten teacher. *The Urban Review.* https://doi.org/10.1007/s11256-020-00577-9

Darling-Hammond, L., Holtzman, D. J., Gatlin, S. J., & Heilig, J. V. (2005). Does teacher preparation matter? Evidence about teacher certification, Teach for America, and teacher effectiveness. *Education Policy Analysis Archives, 13*(42), 1–51.

Ellis, A. L., & Hartlep, N. D. (2017). Struggling in silence: A qualitative study of six African American male stutterers in educational settings. *The Journal of Educational Foundations, 30*(1–4), 33–62.

Howard, T. C. (2001). Telling their side of the story: African American students' perceptions of culturally relevant teaching. *Urban Review,* 33(2), 131–149.

Ingersoll, R., & Strong, M. (2011). The impact of induction and mentoring for beginning teachers: A critical review of the research. *Review of Educational Research, 81*(2), 201–233.

Irvine, J. J., & Fenwick, L. T. (2011). Teachers and teaching for the new millennium: The role of HBCUs. *Journal of Negro Education, 80*(3), 197–208.

Ladson-Billings, G. (1995). But that's just good teaching! The case for culturally relevant pedagogy. *Theory into practice, 34*(3), 159–165.

Ladson-Billings, G. (2009). *The dreamkeepers: Successful teachers of African American children.* San Francisco, CA: Jossey-Bass.

Milner, H. R., IV. (2011). Culturally relevant pedagogy in a diverse urban classroom. *Urban Review, 43*(1), 66–89.

Paris, D., & Alim, S. (Eds.). (2017). *Culturally sustaining pedagogies: Teaching and learning for justice in a changing world.* New York, NY: Teachers College Press.

Siddle Walker, V. (2001). African American teaching in the south: 1940–1960. *American Educational Research Journal, 38*(4), 751–779.

Siddler Walker, V. (2005). Organized resistance and Black educators' quest for school equality, 1878–1938. *Teachers College Record, 107*(3), 355–388.

Wilson, M., & Hallum, P. J. (2006). *Using student achievement test scores as evidence of external validity for indicators of teacher quality: Connecticut's Beginning Educator Support and Training program.* Berkeley: University of California at Berkeley.

CHAPTER 2

TURNING UP WITH THE TORCH

The Transformational Power of a Legacy of Male "Warm Demanders"

Anthony Broughton

Amid the oftentimes drab nature of daily desk work, the soothing sound of Mr. Joseph Brown's keyboard in my elementary music class imbued upon me a passion for music in the classroom. As my first Black male educator, Mr. Brown affirmed my affinity for music as early as first grade. He was my "other father" (Lynn, Bacon, Totten, Bridges, & Jennings, 2010; Milner, 2013) in school, who would often say, "I'm watching you Broughton!" Although he is not the focus of this chapter, and I do not remember many details from my early childhood experiences, I do recall that he was very attentive. As a child I believed that he possessed eyes in the back of his head because he could see my every move. Consequently, I strove to always make Mr. Brown proud; because he paid attention to me; and ensured I was always being and doing my best. This made me feel valued and visible, because he "saw" me. Mr. Brown and I had something in common. We were both

The Impact of Classroom Practices, pages 7–18

former students of Mr. Mack Guice, II. Mr. Guice was my middle and high school music instructor who "told" me what I was going to become; and what I was "going" to do to get there. As custom for many African American educators historically (Foster, 1994), Mr. Guice demanded excellence; and consistently devoted his time and energy to mandating that I "drew forth" my own potential. Educare is the root word for education, which means to "draw forth." Thus, Mr. Guice's ability to draw out my potential made him an "educator," rather than just "teacher." Mr. Guice cultivated a seed (me); and now he is able to see the fruits of his contribution to the collective labor of my community.

Mr. Guice was what Delpit (2012) considers a "warm demander"; one who would "expect a great deal of their students, convince them of their own brilliance, and help them to reach their potential in a disciplined and structured environment" (p. 77). He demanded that we were always attentive, conscious, and astute; and held us accountable for information that was provided to or by us. Mr. Guice and Mr. Brown were both staples in our community; and well revered by many students, parents, teachers, and community members. Drawing from Delpit's concept of "warm demanders," I reflect and share "teachable moments" through vignettes from one of my only Black male educators, that have shaped my educator identity and educational philosophy. Music was the common thread, as the torch of excellence was passed from one Black male educator to the next. I demonstrate how Mr. Guice's verbal and non-verbal communication styles and passion for music in the classroom made a lasting impression on me. I reflect on how their work inspired me to become an educator who "turned up" with music in the classroom. Finally, I provide recommendations for "educators," teachers, preservice teachers, and teacher educators, which conceptualizes Black male educators as "more than just male bodies in the classroom" (Bryan & Williams, 2017).

I became an educator like Mr. Guice. I was not afraid to "turn up" in my classroom, because I understood the transformative power of music. I understood that it was my responsibility to continue his legacy and the legacy of Mr. Brown by passing the torch to the next generation. Mr. Guice has influenced my teacher identity, and my conceptions of the roles of Black men in the classroom. Inspired by Oprah Winfrey's (2014), *What I know for sure,* I share proven practices I have learned from Mr. Guice through experiences. These practices or approaches are *proven,* not only because I have experienced them first hand in Mr. Guice's class, or because I have experienced them in my own class as a teacher, but because "research" has demonstrated that it has yielded favorable results. This is particularly essential because practices that have historically been employed in U.S. classrooms have *proven* to be effective for most White American children, and culturally irrelevant for children of color (Ladson-Billings, 2006). Thus, my voice, as a Black male educator, having been "schooled" in U.S. schools (Woodson, 1933) is essential; because the narratives, experiences, and ways of knowing and being Black male educators and Black students have traditionally been omitted, marginalized, or silenced in dominant discourse regarding pedagogy in U.S. schools. Thus, I will share what "I" know for sure, after reflecting upon Mr. Guice's practice. I use the term, "warm demander" in this chapter to describe Mr. Mack Guice, II because he "cared" (Gay, 2010) and *proved* that we could achieve and exceed all expectations, when provided "spaces and relationships where ethnically diverse students feel recognized, respected, valued, seen, and heard" (Gay, 2010, p. 51).

TEACHING WITH PASSION: PENTACOSTAL PEDAGOGY IN MR. GUICES' CLASS

Warm demanders

> see themselves as advocates for the young people within a system that may not be so caring. They adopt many of the attributes of parents. They consider the whole child, not just his or her mind. They are concerned with the kind of people they are helping to mold—they focus on promoting character, honesty, responsibility, respect, creativity, and kindness. (Delpit, 2012, p. 85)

I have also seen "miracles performed" by warm demanders, but none like that of Mr. Mack Guice, II—an African American male, native of Birmingham, Alabama. He wore black shades, a black beret, and was always dressed to impress. He wore a ring with the Mercedes Benz icon that matched his car; and proudly threw up "hooks" (both of his hands raised up to the sides of his head turned outwards), holding his bald head high, to represent his fraternity, Omega Psi Phi. He was and still is highly revered amongst our rural community. He walked with authority; bearing a bachelor's and master's degree. Although he was a renaissance man and a multitalented educator who could do it all; teaching music was something he was passionate about.

Learning in many of my classrooms as a student was primarily centered around textbooks. Many students became passive learners (Hammond, 2014), having been indoctrinated with content written through Eurocentric cultural lens (Boutte, 2016; Hammond, 2014; Paris, 2012). I was a droid in these textbook driven classrooms; harboring my inner potential, artistic abilities, ideas, and creativity by "listening" and "being quiet" to navigate the oftentimes Eurocentric culture of school (Boutte, 2016; Dubois, 1903; Hammond, 2014; Paris, 2012). I was *"young, gifted, and Black"* (Perry, Steele, & Hilliard, 2003), but could have easily been "labeled" as dis-engaged. This was because pedagogy in these classrooms were disengaging. However, pedagogy in Mr. Guice's class was liberating, because he spoke to our needs; and needs we did not know we possessed. His firm grip on content knowledge, and charismatic and relevant approach to content delivery, oftentimes made me want to shout, "preach!" In fact, I would oftentimes say, "preach" in class, when he made statements that resonated with me. Mr. Guice integrated life skills into his lessons that spoke to our experiences. Thus, I would describe the delivery style of Mr. Guice's instruction as what Emdin (2016) refers to as Pentecostal pedagogy. Mr. Guice often prompted my peers and I to reflect about our performance through his consistent questioning techniques. The very first concept Mr. Guice taught in each class was the art of listening. He would inquire, "Class, what is listening?" He expected us to respond in unison, "Listening is being able to respond to what has been said or heard." He believed that you would be unable to appropriately respond if you were not listening; and rather than chastise us when we did not follow directions, Mr. Guice would inquire, "Class, what is listening?" We would have to pause and recite the definition that he taught us to reinforce his expectations.

This usage of call and response (Smitherman, 1986) as an approach to teaching and building a sense of community still resonates with me. When he spoke certain phrases, he expected that we responded in unison. This is the same approach that we used as drum majors to manage and communicate with our peers on the marching band. When we said, "Band attention!" the band members replied, "CHS!" The call and response was our primary mode of communication; and primary method of getting everyone's attention. We also used call and response to recite spirit chants, which were done collectively. What I know for sure is that teachers should use call and response for instruction and to build a sense of community.

CULTURALLY RELEVANT APPROACHES

I struggled the first two weeks learning to play a note on my trumpet, because I had not mastered the blowing technique. That changed when Mr. Guice told me to "spit the grits." I instantly blew my first note upon employing his strategy. His strategy was culturally relevant to me because I enjoyed eating grits; and connected effortlessly with the concept. Mr. Guice also used mnemonic devices to teach us how to read music. To date, I recall Mr. Guice using "elephants got big dirty feet," "every good boy does fine," and "FACE" as a strategy to 'read' notes on the music staff. As a result, I learned how to read music and rapidly traversed through the band ranks to drum major. What I know for sure is that mnemonic devices that resonate with students and culturally relevant strategies support learning.

Mr. Guice also fostered culturally relevant learning through his approach to musical literacies. He affirmed our interests by teaching us how to read, write, and transpose some of our favorite rap, gospel, and R&B songs. He made learning and reading music meaningful and relevant, because he listened and learned about our interests and values. As a result, we developed the skill to read and play music across multiple genres; while developing cultural competence. "Our music" (hip-hop) was affirmed, and not seen as the "Black noise" that Rose (1994) articulated. This contributed to the positive rapport and sense of community that he fostered, because he demonstrated he "cared" by integrating our values in the curriculum. What I know for sure is that teachers must listen and learn about student's interests and values, and integrate it in a meaningful fashion.

A COMMUNITY-CENTERED EDUCATOR

Mr. Guice was prominent in the community. Everyone knew him; and those who did not know him personally, knew of him. It was common to encounter him in the grocery store, gas station, church, or at a community event, even though he did not live in our community. The high school marching band was highly revered in the community; with a rich legacy, under Mr. Guices' tutelage. From Day 1, Mr. Guice made it known that he knew who I was, and everything about me (hooks, 2004). "Anthony Broughton! I know exactly who you are," were the first words he said to me. I immediately felt affirmed (Gay, 2010). I discovered that Mr. Guice knew who I was, because he also taught my mother and father when they were in school, as members of the marching band. My mother was a majorette, and my father was a drummer; so I knew that joining the band would be an approach to continue their legacy. I knew up front that Mr. Guice was serious business, because of the longevity, and stability he provided our band program. Mr. Joseph Brown, my first Black male teacher, who taught music had a very unique connection to this storyline. He was also my mother and father's classmate, and a student of Mr. Mack Guice, II. This speaks to the level of interconnectivity that Mr. Guice had with not only his students, but the community. He saw teaching as a way to give back to the community, so he spent a great deal of time cultivating us by using various approaches to "draw out" our potential. What I know for sure is that educators must get to know students and their families.

BEYOND THE CLASSROOM WALLS

Mr. Guice was deliberate in what he exposed us to. He was passionate and adamant about exposing us to the possibilities of higher education. Although we thought we were simply rehearsing solely to march in college homecoming parades, looking back I realize that these experiences were so significant to my interest in college. We did not realize that Mr. Guice was intentionally exposing us to college. We toured the campuses and attended football games after the college homecoming parades. Although we attended several college homecoming parades, the annual homecoming experience at Benedict College left an everlasting impression on me. Thus, by my senior year in high school, I was adamant that Benedict College was the best choice for me. Unlike other seniors at the time, I did not have to do a campus tour, or research information about the college because of the co-curricular opportunities Mr. Guice afforded me through the marching band. Additionally, he supported us in going to band camp at Johnson C. Smith University for two summers, which transformed my life and taught me discipline. As a result, my peers and I discovered leadership skills we never knew we possessed; and we were able to employ those skills to strengthen our band program when we returned from camp. What I know for sure is that effective educators must foster meaningful learning and personal development opportunities beyond the walls of the classroom.

SHARED RESPONSIBILITY

I do not recall any major discipline issues in Mr. Guice's class. We had great reverence for him; and disrespecting him in any way was inconceivable. There were a handful of my peers over the course of my 7 years under Mr. Guice's tutelage, that I witnessed a student test Mr. Guice. We knew he did not tolerate disrespect, but there were always a few who would test the waters to discover the consequences of disrespect that most of us were too apprehensive to consider. The first time I witnessed Mr. Guice discipline a student was during a band class when I was in the eighth grade. It involved a male student who refused to pull up his pants. At the time, the school had a strict dress code policy in an attempt to prepare us for the "professional" world, which was outlined in our student handbook. Our shirts had to be pulled up and tucked at all times. However, during this particular day, there was one student in our class who refused to comply with the dress code policy.

We were all warming up our instruments, preparing for the lesson, and we heard one of our male peers shout, "I ain't pullin up nothing!" after Mr. Guice asked him to adhere to the dress code. "What did you just say?" inquired Mr.Guice, leaning in toward the student with his eyes squinted, as if he misunderstood what he uttered. We were aghast. "I *said,* I ain't pullin up nothing," reiterated the student. To our dismay, Mr. Guice calmly said with assertiveness (Brown, 2004), "Step into my office." We did not hear yelling, or screaming. Moments later, our classmate exited the office with his pants pulled up, with a different attitude. He came back and sat down in the seat and complied the remainder of the period. There was no evidence that an incident had occurred. I always marveled at the transformative nature of Mr. Guice's individualized student meetings. He never disciplined students in the presence of their peers. He would always say, "Step in my office" or "Let me have a word with you." This approach did not embarrass us; but rather fostered an opportunity for dialogue. Thus, we perceived this approach as a demonstration of Mr. Guice's respect for us as young adults. Unlike the dehumanizing approaches commonly employed by most teachers, where students were chastised amid their peers, we were treated by Mr. Guice as a key player in the decision making process. Mr. Guice's approach was effective because he understood as outlined by Brown (2004) that

> Power struggles between teachers and students often result in more hostility and a complete lack of respect between the two. It is wise for teachers to avoid power struggles initiated by students. Students have power, and as they enter middle school and advance to high school their power base increases as they attempt to impress peers and other classmates by initiating arguments with teachers. (p. 284)

Mr. Guice protected students from embarrassment, because otherwise our peers would have witnessed us lose the power struggle. Power struggles did not exist with Mr. Guice because he had zero tolerance for disrespect; especially since he always respected and went above and beyond for us. As underscored by Delpit (1995), "Black children expect an authority figure to act with authority" (p. 35). Mr. Guice did not make requests, or provide us with options that did not mirror our potential or our worth. He did not allow us to disrespect him, ourselves, or our families. Rather than regarding him as an authority figure for the sake of doing what he said to do, because he said it; we regarded him as a father or school guardian who strived to protect us. Lynn (2006) referred to this relationship as "other fathering," which is a mixture of "tough love, discipline, and caring" (p. 2517). We knew this because Mr. Guice "saved" us from school suspension, and the "pipeline" to prison (Perry, Steele, & Hilliard, 2003) that we may have otherwise become victims of. We knew he truly loved and cared for and about us; because he demonstrated love through his actions. It felt good to see a "strong" Black man love the way he did (hooks, 2004). He immediately (Brown, 2004) resolved issues rather than passing it down to the administrators; because of his level of accountability for us. What we now know for sure is that "children don't care how much you know, until they know how much you care." When children know that you care they will do anything to demonstrate a high level of respect toward you.

Mr. Guice cared by protecting us—as much as he could, from the "pipeline to prison" (Perry, Steele, & Hilliard, 2003; Wright & Counsell, 2018). This act of "caring" spoke to his ability to foster meaningful personal and interpersonal relationships with his students and members of the community (Boutte, 2016; Gay, 2010; Hammond, 2014). He possessed what Hilliard (1991) referred to as the "will" to ensure we succeeded by implementing collective responsibility, which others may refer to as "classroom management." We were never oblivious of Mr. Guice's expectations, because he was clear and transparent with his expectations and intentions (Ware, 2006) for us on the first day of class. Not only was he explicit in his expectations, he also discussed class norms, and modeled the behavior he expected (Metropolitan Center for Urban Education, 2008). We felt like we belonged because we had a sense of ownership through the various leadership roles he assigned us, such as "trumpet section leader"; so we "managed" our class. What I know for sure is that students should have leadership opportunities in the learning space to reinforce the concept of collective responsibility.

LEARNING FROM LEGACIES

There were photos of former band and choir members (our parents, cousins, and community members) that adorned the classroom walls. These photos reminded us of the legacy we were charged to uphold and advance. Mr. Guice oftentimes told us stories about previous band members, and how things were "back in the day." Oral histories were a key aspect of our classroom learning (King & Swartz, 2014; Long, Baines, & Tisdale, 2018). It supported us in developing a sense of pride for our heritage. Ladson-Billings (1995, 2009) referred to this as developing cultural competence. What I know for sure is that students should see their cultural and historical legacies depicted in the curriculum and classroom environment.

Mr. Guice also showed us videos that modeled certain skills he wanted us to develop. He had voluminous VHS tape recordings of what we referred to as "historical" band drills. While the videos supported visual learners like myself, this culturally sustaining approach (Paris, 2012) also provided us an opportunity to "learn from the past." Mr. Guice created a group of student leaders called band council, which comprised of all the instrument section leaders. We met daily to discuss ideas, issues, and to plan instruction for the entire band. Upon watching the VHS tapes he converted to DVD, we learned (Hew & Brush, 2007) "the chocolate butter milk" from a university marching band that Mr. Guice filmed. Through a series of co-generative dialogues (Emdin, 2011), the band council integrated the chocolate butter milk into our half-time performance and developed a plan to teach the moves to the band. Since Mr. Guice did not teach moves, we learned how to teach various types of learners during this process (Gardner, 2006; Silver, 2005). Students who did not attend rehearsal, learn the music, or had discipline or academic issues were required to stand on the sidelines of the field during our half-time performance. Therefore, we all learned discipline. Mr. Guice's expectations were high; and the videos of past band performances reminded us of why he set the bar so high. Mr. Guice wanted us to be great; so he always showed us images and videos of greatness. This strategy influenced our behavior, because we knew that Mr. Guice believed in us. What I know for sure is that students should have the opportunity to teach and learn from their peers. This requires that teachers allow students to take ownership of learning, by relinquishing "dominant control" over student learning (Friere, 1970).

BROTHER TO BROTHER

As a current educator, I always speak to my students individually regarding discipline concerns, because I remember how respected I felt to know that Mr. Guice would never humiliate me in the presence of my peers. Although Mr. Guice fostered meaningful rapports with students in the classroom, he also taught us "brotherhood" through his mentoring group (Lynn, Bacon, Totten, Bridges, & Jennings, 2010). We did not believe that Mr. Guice ever slept. Although Mr. Guice committed himself to teaching and being a band and choir director, he was also a mentor. Mr. Guice, myself, and two other peers established the Omega Team fraternity, a high school mentoring group and step team influenced by Mr. Guice's fraternity, Omega Psi Phi. This mentoring group and step team cultivated brotherhood and taught us the value of collaboration, perseverance, and community service. Although this group made a positive impact on my peers and I during high school, I was inspired by Alpha Phi Alpha Fraternity, Incorporated to take my intellectual acumen to new heights. Thus, I developed a mentoring group and step team when I became an educator to stimulate the intellectual abilities of the male students in my school. What I know for sure is that mentoring groups and school step teams provide a positive outlet and a communal space to foster personal and professional development.

Mr. Guice's approach to supporting our personal and professional development made him an ideal model for an educator, or elder (King & Swartz, 2014), who cultivated his students holistically. He was truly what Broughton (2019) referred to as a green thumb educator. Like plants, we were all diverse, but Mr. Guice had the ability to identify our needs and provide us with opportunities that helped us bloom. What I know for sure is that "the best teachers show you where to look, but don't tell you what to see." Mr. Guice always told us where to look, but never what to see. We were afforded the freedom to think for ourselves and to go against the grain so that we would not become passive learners (Hammond, 2014). He gave us autonomy, but also preached shared responsibility (King, 2014, 2018).

RECOMMENDATIONS FOR PRACTICE

- Children do not care how much you know, until they know how much you care.
- Effective educators must foster meaningful learning and personal development opportunities beyond the classroom (Boutte & Hill, 2006).
- Students should see their cultural and historical legacies depicted in the curriculum and classroom environment (Gay, 2010).
- Mentoring groups and school step teams provide a positive outlet and a communal space to foster personal and professional development (Lynn, Bacon, Totten, Bridges, & Jennings, 2010).
- Educators must foster a sense of community and shared responsibility.
- Educators must develop relationships with students to intentionally integrate their interests and values into the curriculum.
- Educators must get to know students and their families (Boutte, 2016; Boutte & Hill, 2006).

REFERENCES

Broughton, A. (2019). *Evidence-based approaches to becoming a culturally responsive educator: Emerging research and opportunities.* Hershey, PA: IGI Global.

Boutte, G. S., & Hill, E. L. (2006). African American communities: Implications for education. *New Educator, 2*, 311–329.

Boutte, G. S. (2016). *Educating African American students: And how are the children?* New York, NY: Routledge.

Brown, D. F. (2004). Urban teachers' professed classroom management strategies. *Urban Education, 39*(3), 266–289.

Bryan, N., & Milton Williams, T. (2017). We need more than just male bodies in classrooms: Recruiting and retaining culturally relevant black male teachers in early childhood education. *Journal of Early Childhood Teacher Education, 38*(3), 209–222.

Delpit, L. (1995). *Other people's children: Cultural conflict in the classroom.* New York, NY: New Press.

Delpit, L. (2012). *"Multiplication is for White people": Raising expectations for other people's children.* New York, NY: The New Press.

Du Bois, W. E. B. (1903). *The souls of black folk: Essays and sketches.* Chicago, IL: A.C. McClurg.

Emdin, C. (2011). Moving beyond the boat without a paddle: Reality pedagogy, black youth, and urban science education. *The Journal of Negro Education, 80*(3), 284–295.

Emdin, C. (2016). *For White folks who teach in the hood... and the rest of y'all too: Reality pedagogy and urban education.* Boston, MA: Beacon Press.

Foster, M. (1994). Effective black teachers: A literature review. In E. Hollins, J. King, & W. Hayman (Eds), *Teaching diverse populations: Formulating a knowledge base* (pp. 225–242). Albany: State University of New York Press.

Freire, P. (1970). *Pedagogy of the Oppressed.* London, England: Penguin

Gardner, H. (2006). *The development and education of the mind.* New York, NY: Routledge.

Gay, G. (2010). *Culturally responsive teaching: Theory, research, and practice.* New York, NY: Teachers College Press.

Hammond, Z. L. (2014). *Culturally responsive teaching and the brain: Promoting authentic engagement and rigor among culturally and linguistically diverse students* (1st ed.). Thousand Oaks, CA: Corwin.

Hew, K. F., & Brush, T. (2007). Integrating technology into K–12 teaching and learning: Current knowledge gaps and recommendations for future research. *Educational Technology Research & Development, 55*(3), 223–252.

Hilliard, A. G., III. (1991). Do we have the will to educate all children? *Educational Leadership, 49*(1), 31–36.

hooks, b. (2004). *We real cool: Black men and masculinity.* New York, NY: Routledge.

King, J. E., & Swartz, E. E. (2014). *"Re-membering" history in student and teacher learning: An Afrocentric culturally informed praxis.* New York, NY: Routledge.

King, J. E., & Swartz, E. E. (2018). *Heritage knowledge in the curriculum: Retrieving an African Episteme.* New York, NY: Routledge.

Ladson-Billings, G. (1995). Toward a theory of culturally relevant pedagogy. American *Educational Research Journal, 32*(3), 465–491. https://doi.org/10.2307/1163320

Ladson-Billings, G. (2006). From the achievement gap to the education debt: Understanding achievement in U.S. schools. *Educational Researcher, 35*(7). 3–12.

Ladson-Billings, G. (2009). *The dreamkeepers: Successful teachers of African American children* (2nd ed.). San Francisco, CA: Jossey-Bass.

Long, S., Baines, J., & Tisdale, C. (2018). *"We've been doing it your way long enough": Choosing the culturally relevant classroom.* New York, NY: Teachers College Press.

Lynn, M. (2006). Dancing between two worlds: Portrait of the life of a Black male teacher in South Central L.A. *International Journal of Qualitative Studies in Education, 19*(2), 221–242.

Lynn, M., Bacon, J. N., Totten, T. L., Bridges, T. L., III., & Jennings, M. (2010). Examining teachers' beliefs about African American male students in a low-performing high school in an African American school district. *Teachers College Record, 112*(1), 289–330.

Metropolitan Center for Urban Education. (2008). *Culturally responsive classroom management strategies.* Retrieved from http://steinhardt.nyu.edu/scmsAdmin/uploads/005/121/Culturally%20Responsive%20Classroom%20Mgmt%20Strat2.pdf

Milner, H. (2013). Chapter five: A talk to teachers about Black male students. *Counterparts, 383,* 67–85.

Paris, D. (2012). Culturally sustaining pedagogy: A needed change in stance, terminology, and practice. *Educational Researcher, 41*(3), 93–97.

Perry, T., Steele, C., & Hilliard, A., III. (2003). *Young, gifted, and Black: Promoting high achievement among African American students.* Boston, MA: Beacon Press.

Rose, T. (1994). *Black Noise: Rap music and Black culture in contemporary America.* Middletown, CT: Wesleyan University Press.

Silver, D. (2005). *Drumming to the beat of different marchers: Finding the rhythm for differentiated learning.* Nashville, TN: Incentive.

Smitherman, G. (1986). *Talkin and testifyin: The language of Black America.* Detroit, MI: Wayne State University Press.

Ware, F. (2006). Warm demander pedagogy culturally responsive teaching that supports a culture of achievement for African American students. *Urban Education, 41*(4), 427–456. https://doi.org/10.1177/0042085906289710

Winfrey, O. (2014). *What I know for sure.* New York, NY: Flatiron Books.

Woodson, C. G. (1933). *The mis-education of the Negro.* New York, NY: Wilder.

Wright, B. L., Counsell, S. L. (2018). *The brilliance of Black boys: Cultivating school success in the early grades.* New York, NY: Teachers College Press.

CHAPTER 3

INSPIRATION AND MOTIVATION

How One Teacher Changed the Course of My Educational Trajectory

Kenneth D. Brown

THE EARLY YEARS

I was born and mostly raised in Jackson, Mississippi and I am a product of Jackson Public Schools. I understand the racial implications that come with growing up in the Deep South, but I wasn't truly able to conceptualize the disparities until I was an adult residing in other parts of the country. When compared to other states, Mississippi ranks last or close to last in almost every identifiable measure imaginable (poverty, infant mortality rate, STI's, etc.; Michaela, 2018). Jackson, the capital and largest city in the state has an African American population of 82% (World Population Review, 2020). The allocation of resources, or lack thereof, impacted most communities and led to an increase in crime. In the 1980s, neighborhoods in Jackson were still mostly segregated, and students were bussed to schools in different areas to integrate the populations.

The Impact of Classroom Practices, pages 19–28

I started attending Key Elementary School in first grade and would stay through sixth grade. The student population was approximately 60% White and 40% African American at the time. The teaching staff at Key was diverse. During my years of attendance, I had three White female teachers, two African American female teachers, one White male teacher, and two African American male teachers. I enjoyed attending school and was seen as a smart student by teachers and classmates. I was frequently chosen to be the classroom helper. I served on the safety patrol team and was responsible for transporting students to and from the bus and making sure everyone stayed in their seats while the bus was in motion. I even participated in a mock election and out of three positions, I was the only African American elected. I was chosen to write about the experience for our school newspaper and spent time in our gifted and talented classroom. Although I recognized the differences between my White peers and myself, I did not feel as though I was treated differently by most of my teachers at the time because of my race. I did feel that my African American male teachers expected me to act a certain way and they thought that intimidation was the best way to motivate me.

While in elementary school, I also started learning how to play musical instruments. In second grade, I began taking piano lessons. My instructor was African American. He was very kind and always professional. After 2 years of lessons, my excitement wore off and I stopped. Around the same time, I started playing the viola at school. I enjoyed learning how to play the viola and participating in the recital, but the teacher was not memorable. I only played the viola during my fourth-grade year and did not revisit musical instruments until I went to junior high school.

I believe that my perceptions of my classmates' home lives started shaping the way I recognized the differences between the White and Black students. I felt as if all my White classmates resided in the nice houses surrounding the school, with both parents, and had very few issues. Media played a huge part in my perception of my White classmates at the time. In contrast, I saw myself, and classmates who looked like me, leave neighborhoods plagued with decay, to attend our school. We lived in single family homes with our mother and siblings. We were responsible for our younger siblings' safety to and from school as well as after school until our mothers came home from work. Most received government assistance. Where we received free or reduced lunch at school, I saw most of my White friends bringing their lunch or paying full price. I am aware that this is an overgeneralization of the experiences of my White and Black classmates but at the time I felt that I had more in common outside of school with my Black classmates and had more in common at school with my classmates perceived as smart regardless of their skin color.

Overall, I enjoyed my elementary school experience and left believing I was a highly intelligent boy who could accomplish anything. I developed a strong academic foundation. In elementary school, I did not have a relationship with a teacher that pushed me to achieve more. I believe I was motivated by the school-wide incentive program where "key bucks" were given to students based on grades to buy big ticket items such as bikes and stereos, but I was also motivated by a desire to achieve. As I grew older and started to change physically, mentally, and emotionally; what motivated me also changed.

THE START OF JUNIOR HIGH

I started seventh grade at Hardy Junior High, which had a predominately African American population. In this environment, I was able to thrive in a space with peers and teachers who looked like me. As I moved through adolescence, I was becoming increasingly shy. I had a core group of friends and support from teachers that made the transition to junior high seamless though. Academically, I performed well. My classes were not advanced. At the time, I didn't know that advanced level classes other than gifted and talented existed. I earned mostly As and Bs in my classes with little effort being exerted. In seventh grade, I also signed up for band as an elective. I enjoyed the band experience even though I hated playing my instrument. I only played the flute for 1 year, after which I asked my mother to exchange it for the instrument I would grow to love, the saxophone.

I began eighth grade in a junior high that was located in the suburbs. Brandon Junior High was predominately White and reminded me of my days at Key. Although I was only there for a short amount of time, I developed friendships and performed well academically. I do not feel as though I stood out in any way as a student, academically or socially. As I reflect on the time there, if teachers treated me differently or had different expectations for me, it wasn't apparent to me. That changed significantly once I transitioned to my next school.

DARKER DAYS

In October of my eighth-grade year, my family moved back into the city and I attended Siwell Junior High. Siwell's student population was approximately 55% White and 45% African American. There appeared to be an even mix of White teachers and teachers of color. During my eighth and ninth grade years at Siwell, I had 12 teachers. Four of them were men. Three were African American and one was Latinx.

The transition to Siwell was especially difficult for me. Being shy, it was difficult to become acclimated in the new environment especially starting well into the school year. I struggled to become comfortable to interact with my classmates and felt isolated most of the time. I also felt unmotivated in most of my classes. I earned Bs or Cs on most assignments and tests without studying. Most times I wasn't paying attention in the class and still scored well. The material was not challenging, and I did not find it the least bit interesting.

I was also having trouble dealing with challenges at home. My mother remarried and I did not get along with my stepdad. He would discipline me which added to the animosity I felt towards him. To add insult to injury, my body was changing. I grew several inches my eighth-grade year and started putting on size. I felt awkward about the new size and it showed in my disposition. I was extremely unhappy and severely depressed. I felt as if I did not fit in at home or school.

At this point, I realized how easy it was to skip school. I was the last to leave home in the mornings and as long as I came home at the time the bus normally dropped me off, no one would know I missed school. Initially, I would miss days sporadically. It quickly became more frequent and even multiple days in a row. I would stay home watching tv all day and when it was time for my brother to come home, I would leave or hide until 3:30 p.m. One winter day, I even hid in my stepdad's truck that was parked in the driveway for an hour to avoid being caught. My mother, stepdad, aunt, and uncle took turns taking me to school trying to improve my attendance, but I did whatever I could to miss the bus and not go. I hated school. It served no purpose. It did not seem to be preparing me for any type of future and I felt like it was a complete waste of time.

ENTER, MY FAVORITE TEACHER

Things slowly began to change after I started developing a relationship with my band director, Charles Bradley. He was the first to recognize my talent as a musician and cultivated my gift. Through our interactions and conversations, I felt as if I was finally being seen. Mr. Bradley showed me that he not only cared about my ability to master playing the saxophone, but also my overall development as a scholar and a person. He took the time to learn about my genuine interests and what I excelled in.

I immediately noticed the difference between Mr. Bradley's class and the previous classes I had taken. The energy was different. I came into the space well after systems, routines, and relationships had already been established but I felt welcomed as soon as I entered the room. He quickly assessed my musical ability and tailored my instruction to meet my needs. He made learning fun. Although we were learning basic music, he pushed our thinking and helped us to develop our craft. He introduced us to music that students who had more musical experience typically played and challenged us to perform it well.

Mr. Bradley invested time in getting to know me. He asked questions about my home life and kept up with how I was performing in other classes. He also monitored my attendance. Mr. Bradley was the teacher who brought to my mother's attention my attendance issues. He overheard other students discussing my absences one week (I was out Monday and Tuesday of that particular week) and he contacted my mother immediately. Mr. Bradley took the charge of helping me become more acclimated to the school environment to help motivate me to want to be there once I actually arrived. He would take the time to check in to see how I was really doing. Slowly, school started becoming more manageable. He fostered my self-confidence musically which impacted all aspects of my life. Mr. Bradley encouraged me to try out for the all-city band my ninth grade year. Because of his teaching and support, I made the list and was the only baritone saxophone player in the junior high all-city ensemble that year.

Although Mr. Bradley was very supportive, he was no pushover. He had a muscular build with a huge presence. His voice was deep and echoed through the band hall. He would praise us when we performed well and let us know he was proud of us. There were times he would sit back in his seat, smirking and nodding his head in approval of how we sound. But there were other times where he would correct us when needed. Sometimes he would yell and even throw a music stand, but, interestingly enough, I never felt afraid of him. It is thought that the best way to discipline students of color, particularly African American males, is by threatening and yelling at them. While this may work for a lot, it wasn't the best approach for me. I tend to shut down when yelled at which would affect my comfort within that setting as well as my overall performance. My relationship with other teachers who used this tactic would forever be impacted and I would avoid all interactions with them moving forward whenever possible. But because I knew Mr. Bradley genuinely cared about me and wanted me to do my very best, I knew his moments of yelling came from a place of support and was never used to demean me or my peers. He rarely singled students out when scolding them especially when critiquing our performances. In ninth grade, Mr. Bradley challenged me on the way I was behaving in his class. I felt as though I performed better than another student on a solo assignment and voiced my disagreement with his grading. Initially, Mr. Bradley explained his rationale for both grades, but I still didn't think the scores were fair. He then said my performance wasn't as great as I thought it was and that I needed to humble myself about my talents. "It doesn't help to put someone else down to make yourself seem better, and your performance wasn't all that," he exclaimed. I was upset by his feedback but after some self-reflection, I realized he was right. Although I knew I played the saxophone well, there was always room for improvement and always someone who performed better. That little gem has guided me throughout my educational path and career.

Mr. Bradley built a relationship between home and school by communicating with my mother. He told her that I was talented enough to play the saxophone professionally. He would give me rides home after practice, along with other students, in the back of his Toyota 4Runner. I would ask to ride home with him when my mother had already planned to pick me up. My mother would come to parent/teacher conferences and share pictures of me with Mr. Bradley while discussing ways they could support my overall development. I knew based on this connection they were working together to push me which worked as motivation to attend school more. I also knew I had support from Mr. Bradley. He encouraged my mother to help cultivate my musical skills which aided in improving my academic growth. I learned that if I missed too many days of school or my grades were too low, I wouldn't be able to perform. Not being able to participate in performances was not an option. So, I limited the amount of days missed which helped improve my school experience.

As we fostered a mentor–mentee relationship, Mr. Bradley showed me he was someone I could look up to. He was married with children. He attended a Historically Black College and University (HBCU). His presence alone was one of the first introductions I had to African American fraternities. Mr. Bradley was a hardworking man. He encouraged me to develop goals and want more for myself by setting the example. When I left ninth grade, I knew I wanted to attend an HBCU and that my brilliance musically as well as academically would create opportunities for me to do so even during those times when other teachers didn't acknowledge it. For years after I left Siwell I would randomly run into Mr. Bradley. Each time, he would ask me if I still played my instrument. He was always proud to hear that I did and was extremely disappointed when I told him I was no longer in the band while in college. After all the students he's taught over so many years, it always amazed me that he remembered details of my life. Mr. Bradley made me feel special in class and continued to do so for years to come although our interactions were now short and rare.

HIGH SCHOOL AND BEYOND

Mr. Bradley taught me how to be self-motivating. When I went to Forest Hill High School my sophomore year, I remember feeling the same lack of motivation from teachers. I wasn't pushed to think critically and with me now having more height and size added (at this point I was about 6'3" in height), it appeared as though I wasn't expected to be more than a C level student.

But I channeled the life skills Mr. Bradley instilled in me to be my own inspiration. I found myself continuing to excel academically and musically. I made the all-city high school band 2 years in a row and was first chair my senior year. My grades were still mostly Bs and Cs. I decided to take advanced level classes my senior year in preparation for college and started earning As; not from the motivation of teachers or new band directors, but because I wanted higher grades to make my college applications look more appealing.

Mr. Bradley also showed me the type of relationship I needed with teachers moving forward to feel a part of their classrooms. As I attended Jackson State University, I recognized the importance of those relationships as I struggled to acclimate to the college experience. Teachers' perceptions of me played a major part in that acclimation or lack thereof. Because of my height and size, I began to realize that I was thought to be a student athlete and the teachers' stereotypical overgeneralization led them to believe the work was too challenging for me. I also began to recognize those perceptions were based on race and gender as well. Teachers rarely pushed my thinking, which attributed to less than desirable behaviors in class. I would zone out completely or talk with classmates. Professors questioned my understanding of the content when I easily showed mastery. For example, my college algebra professor, who was an African American woman, said, "Can you come to the board and complete this problem? I knew you couldn't." I responded by saying, "I can if you give me a chance." I solved the equation quickly and correctly. She quietly acknowledged my correct answer and moved forward with the lesson. At the end of the class she asked, "What time do you play tonight?" I looked at her, puzzled. She then asked, "You're on the basketball team, right?" I said, "No, I'm not" and left. It was clear to me she associated my lack of interest in her class or her perception of my lack of mathematical skills to me being an "athlete"; tall, athletic, and Black.

CONCLUSION

As I reflect on my personal teaching experience, I realize I incorporated several teaching and relationship building strategies I saw Mr. Bradley use. He created an environment that was culturally responsive to the needs of all students. Gay (2010) recognizes culturally responsive teaching as "using the cultural knowledge, prior experiences, frames of reference, and performance styles of ethnically diverse students to make learning encounters more relevant to and effective for them" (Cole, David, & Jimenez, 2016). Mr. Bradley fostered our relationship by recognizing and acknowledging my individual strengths and built upon those. He also chose music from different genres to help promote cultural identity and understanding. I have built relationships with my students by investing time into learning as much as possible about them and finding common interests. I have developed lessons using scenarios and materials students can relate to promoting the value of individual experiences and how it relates to the diversity found within the classroom. I have also included reading materials from diverse backgrounds and perspectives to promote cultural awareness.

I understand the importance of Mr. Bradley being an African American man. Although I had other African American male teachers who didn't impact me in similar ways, I know that the commonality between a racial and ethnic identity can have a strong impact on student achievement. Reportedly 2% of all public school teachers are African American men (Bristol, 2015; Duncan 2011). As an educator, I continue to ensure my presence throughout my school is prominent so that the African American boys can see someone who looks like them. It was also important for me to provide instruction to them in an effort to adjust the narrative of the Black male perceived in the media and most communities. Teaching is relationship based and teachers of other races can easily impact the learning of African American male students as well, sometimes in ways more impactful than their African American counterparts. Either way, all teachers must build the knowledge, skills, attitudes, dispositions, and orientations to be successful (Banks, 2015; Milner, 2016).

TEACHER PRESERVICE/INSERVICE

Using a critical teaching pedagogy, I found the following are needed for preservice/inservice support of teachers:

1. *Self-reflection.* Who teachers are, what they experience, and the stories they tell often find themselves in the fabric of their work with students (Milner, 2016). Teachers must honestly assess where they are as it relates to appreciating the diversity of people in general, but specifically the students in their classroom in order to provide meaningful and purposeful instruction that meets the needs of all learners (Richards, Brown, & Ford, 2007). They must ascertain what steps they have taken to foster relationships in the classroom and adjust as needed to build those individual connections (Richards et al., 2007). Space during professional development workshops should be created to allow teachers to reflect on their own commitment to diversity within their classrooms. *Listen to the students.* Most times, students will show or tell the teacher exactly what's needed. I have heard students share that in some classes the work is too easy. Others have shared that the teacher doesn't genuinely care. As the teacher, it is our job to adjust our instruction and

actions to make sure the students feel as though they have been heard by ensuring they are a part of the learning experience, their voice is recognized, and lessons are designed to be engaging for all. We can do so by validating students' cultural identity in classroom practices and instructional materials (Richards et al., 2007). Create spaces where students are able to share verbally or anonymously their concerns and develop a plan to address them in a timely manner. Students should also be educated on the diversity of the world around them while equity and mutual respect is promoted (Richards et al., 2007).

2. *Be willing to learn.* Acquire knowledge about the intersections(s) of teacher racial and ethnic identity, curriculum, and the social context of teaching and learning (Milner, 2016). Learn about personal and family histories and the history and experiences of diverse groups to cultivate an appreciation of diversity (Richards et al., 2007). Create professional development opportunities at the school, online, and offsite related to racial and ethnic identity and diversity. Book studies would also be a great way to gain knowledge on this subject.
3. *Challenge students.* Students must be motivated to become active participants in their learning, encouraged to think critically, and assessed validly (Richards et al., 2007). During my educational experience, I was not challenged academically or pushed to think critically until college. Personal biases must be confronted head on so that students are exposed to the type of instruction they require and deserve. Administration should ensure content planning and lesson development is differentiated based on student culture, identity, and ability.
4. *Foster an "it takes a village" mentality.* Mr. Bradley was a part of my community. He communicated with my mother and other teachers. I saw him in spaces outside of school. His presence in areas that reached farther than the band hall helped me feel as though he was more than just my teacher, but a part of my life. It is important that teachers foster positive interrelationships among students, their families, the community, and school (Richards et al., 2007). This perspective aids teachers in developing lessons that encapsulates different areas of the students' lives into learning while promoting interest in the content. Teachers are encouraged to develop systems that promote regular communication with parents and the community. As a teacher, I have used daily trackers to monitor student interactions by purposefully planning for conversations between select students. I would also suggest teachers participate

in different school-wide initiatives that address diversifying student experiences while promoting a sense of community.

REFERENCES

Banks, J. A. (2015). *Cultural diversity and education: Foundations, curriculum and teaching* (6th ed.). Boston, MA: Pearson.

Bristol, T. (2015, April 28). *Black male teachers: There aren't enough of them* [Web log post]. Retrieved from https://www.washingtonpost.com/news/answer-sheet/wp/2015/04/28/black-male-teachers-there-arent-enough-of-them/

Cole, M. W., David, S. S., & Jiménez, R.T. (2016). Collaborative translation: Negotiating student investment in culturally responsive pedagogy. *Language Arts, 93*(6), 430–443.

Duncan, A. (2011, December 10). *Leading a life of consequence.* Winter commencement speech presented at Fayetteville State University, Fayetteville, NC.

Gay, G. (2010). *Culturally responsive teaching: Theory, research, and practice.* New York, NY: Teachers College Press.

Michaela, G. M. (2018, August 8). Analysis: Mississippi has most underprivileged kids. *TCA Regional News.* Retrieved from https://www.djournal.com/lifestyle/health/analysis-mississippi-has-most-underprivileged-kids/article_107a225d-0929-5a58-96ec-6321a951e688.html

Milner, H. R. (2016). A black male teacher's culturally responsive practices. *The Journal of Negro Education, 85*(4), 417–432.

Richards, H. V., Brown, A. F., & Forde, T. B. (2007). Addressing Diversity in Schools: Culturally Responsive Pedagogy. *TEACHING Exceptional Children, 39*(3), 64–68. https://doi.org/10.1177/004005990703900310

World Population Review. (2020). *Jackson, Mississippi population 2020.* Retrieved from http://worldpopulationreview.com/us-cities/jackson-ms/

CHAPTER 4

DEFYING MEDIA STEREOTYPES

Resilience and Inspiration Fostered by an African American Teacher

Chaz T. Gipson

The goal for this chapter is to highlight how an urban teacher positively changed my life through her unique teaching strategies. She empowered other educators to impact their students with a firm, but fair approach. I will highlight her impact on my life as a current educator and educational leader, despite the negative stereotypes of African American males, portrayed in mass media. Effective teaching strategies highlighted in this chapter will serve as a toolkit from which all preservice and in-service teacher practitioners can utilize to create a dynamic learning atmosphere. In this chapter, I will share how her strong approach to teaching created a space for highly effective learning. Moreover, this chapter is grounded in culturally relevant pedagogy, drawing on connections between my teacher's pedagogical practices and the work of a prominent scholar (Ladson-Billings, 1994).

Today's mass media, comprised of television, social media, radio, newspapers, magazines, and similar sources of news and information, influence

The Impact of Classroom Practices, pages 29–39

how people perceive the varied cultures of the world. Media sources perpetuate or contribute to negative stereotypes of specific populations or groups, particularly African American males (Gipson, 2018). According to Rapport, Bolden, Kolfer, and Savier (2009), African American males must handle unavoidable challenges such as, but not limited to, street violence, educational inequality, burdens that are perpetuated by social, economic, and cultural orientation, and mass media stereotypes. Researchers have posited that the media strongly misrepresents African American males as incarcerated, poor, unemployed, and intellectually challenged, without educational achievement (Adkins-Coleman, 2010; Coakley, 2013). Furthermore, academic success is influenced by socioeconomic environment, poor housing, overcrowding, a shortage of material resources, and the physical placement and conditions of schools (Coakley, 2013).

I come from a social background often represented in such negative portrayals. Having personally experienced an array of challenges and finding my own resilience in community dynamics that served to empower my resistance to them, this urban African American teacher taught me how to overcome challenges with negative media representations to defy media stereotypes. Additionally, I learned how to tenaciously confront personal, social, and academic barriers to achieve academic success. As an educator and educational leader, I have dedicated my life to leading by example and cultivating culturally based resilience through my teachings, research and leadership, and overcoming negative media portrayals of African American males.

In this chapter, first, I introduce readers to the early stages of my life and share some of the challenges that I encountered in a low-income urban environment, particularly the disconnections I had with teachers. Then, I describe my high school years and my introduction to Ms. Hixson. I share in a rich and detailed manner the high expectations that Ms. Hixson demanded and how adhering to her standards helped me get to the place where I am today. As we journey further, I share how we built a relationship through watching an episode of *Oprah* that focused on Morehouse College. I share how Ms. Hixson helped me believe that I can become a Morehouse Man. In my final section, I offer recommendations and strategies that can be helpful for preservice and in-service teachers to positively impact the lives of their students. I hope the narrative shared and the recommendations made will encourage current and future teachers to have the magic of Ms. Hixson.

PRELUDE TO THE OPRAH CONNECTION

"Ms. Hixson, I need help! I am failing, and I can't get an F! I will be kept back, and I will not be able to graduate or go to college. Please help me!"

"Ummm, it's 4 o'clock, I'm off the clock, and it's time for me to watch *The Oprah Winfrey Show.* You should have done what you were supposed to do before now. You need to make an appointment. *Oprah* is on now. Bye!"

As tears rolled down my face, I was beyond shocked. I had been denied help. My teacher had told me that she would rather watch *Oprah* than help me. Still in shock, I told the teacher that my mom and I watched *Oprah* all the time. I asked to watch with her! Hesitantly, she agreed. This was the start of a relationship that changed my life forever.

The *Oprah* episode that we watched together was about being a "Morehouse Man." That episode showed me that I could be more than what the media often portray: A Black male from a low-class urban environment, who accomplishes very little. However, because of Ms. Hixson and watching that episode of *Oprah,* my life, as an educator, has been enriched by the lessons I learned. I also learned that I did not have to conform to the negative portrayals of African American males, as depicted in mass media, and I had what it took to be resilient and defy media stereotypes.

EARLY CHALLENGES

I grew up in a single-parent home in Carver Homes/West End, South Atlanta. The area was generally referred to as "the hood." The neighborhood was filled with crime. Many went to jail. No one was expected to "make it." While I had few positive role models, I knew that this was not the life that I wanted (Gipson, 2019). I faced the usual challenges that young African Americans from lower-income backgrounds encounter. I was the product of a single mother and had no father figure. My community was often plagued with school dropouts, low standardized test scores, high suspension and expulsion rates, and high incarceration rates were the norm. In school, I was picked on, teased, and bullied by the "cool kids." I did not fit in with the "regular kids." I was a church boy, a mama's boy, and a nerd (Gipson, 2019).

Not only was I challenged to make connections with my peers, I was often challenged to make connections with my teachers. I directed much of my energy toward being the stereotypical Black male as a problem child, class clown, a "wannabe thug," and a prodigal son. I was different, and I felt ignored by my teachers. For example, I recalled standing outside a classroom witnessing a teacher fussing at one of her "problem children." She opened the door so aggressively that she unintentionally hit me in the head. Her reaction was, "Oh, I am so sorry, you'll be all right." She immediately turned her attention back to the "problem child." The fact that I was bleeding appeared not to be a concern. Moreover, the teacher's casual reaction to having injured me with, "You'll be all right," caused me both physical and emotional pain. The cut to my forehead was temporary, but the cut to my self-esteem was long term. I was impacted and lost the ability to dream, and the magic of possibilities.

HIGH SCHOOL AND MS. HIXSON

A typical day in this school included suspensions (at least 15 per week), students smoking weed in the bathroom, students being expelled for bringing a weapon on campus, teachers being fired for having sexual relations with other teachers or students, teachers being overwhelmed and leaving in the middle of the semester, or administration hiring unqualified persons as long-term substitutes in critical subject matter courses. Teaching for these individuals consisted of simply babysitting and watching movies like *Set It Off* and/or *The Nutty Professor.*

Then there was Ms. Camela Hixon, my American literature teacher in the 11th grade. She was different. Her no-nonsense approach was unlike other teachers, especially younger teachers, who made overt attempts to be friends with students by trying to be hip or cool but did not necessarily have high or any expectations for students. However, as we entered Ms. Hixson's classroom on the first day, she told us:

> I do not know you or what you are used to. However, welcome to my world. This is a real class and you will do real work. You will earn everything, and nothing will be given to any of you. I do not care who you are, who your momma is, who your daddy is, how cute you think you are. I am the law in here. If I were you, I would dot my I's and cross my T's. Good Luck!

I knew at that point that I was in for a whirlwind. I had never experienced anyone who was that strict and direct. I did not expect to make it through the first week.

Dealing with Ms. Hixson's dominating personality was challenging. Not only was she difficult, she was meticulous about everything. As an English teacher, she had lots of explicit "over-the-top" expectations for students' work. She often used a special phrase: "Hint Hint Clue Clue." It was literally a hint and a clue that whatever she was about to say was important. In fact, she said it so often that you were led to believe that everything was important. She gave very specific instructions:

> Make sure you take notes, no matter what; make sure you always have a blue or black ink pen only in my class. Take notes from the time you awake to the time you leave my class as if your life depends on it, because I am only saying stuff once; if you miss it, you just miss it. Even if it is movie day, take detailed notes. Do not ever forget your textbook, even when you think you don't need it for the day. Make sure your heading is on the left. Always read the side of

> the board when you walk in. There is always a "Do Now" assignment waiting on you. Show up every day, and if you ever even think about skipping class, you will hate life. Do all homework assignments, as they are worth as much as the exams. Take time to organize your notebook for this class and do not throw any papers away. Be prepared for absolutely anything and everything, including a pop quiz, notebook check, textbook check, knowledge check, definition check, homework comprehension check.

Not only did she say these things, she implemented these concepts and penalized us when we forgot. I had a hard time adjusting to this level of perfection. I had never met a teacher who was this "hands on" or who gave us this much work. She piled on writing assignments, homework, reading, quizzes, and exams to the point that we thought we had post-traumatic stress disorder.

Ms. Hixson also had a sense of strict humor and quick wit. She had no problem in reminding students, "Yes, I need a job, but I don't need this job. So, try me if you want, and you will lift up your eyes." We did not know what that meant. Was she going to pray for us? Was she going to hug us? Was she going to pick us up and throw us out the window?

Research suggests that students in urban schools are more motivated to perform classroom tasks when two particular elements co-exist: (a) teachers who set high expectations for student learning and ensure that students meet those expectations, and (b) teachers who build community based on trust and care (Adkins-Coleman, 2010). While I did not always agree with some of Ms. Hixson's strategies, eventually they became the norm, and we quickly adjusted and adapted to meet or exceed her expectations. She met us where we were, made us rise to her standards, and moved us beyond where we believed we could go. She instilled discipline, respect, and tenacity. She exposed us to things that we could not imagine.

In addition to teaching the standard English literature curriculum, Ms. Hixson made it a priority to expose us to college. In our low-income urban environment, college was not in the plans for most students. Most of the students' parents had no experience in or even knowledge of higher education. Ms. Hixson taught us how to construct a résumé, stressing that it was often the first impression for a potential employer. Furthermore, she provided many college preparation assignments by embedding them in the 11th-grade English language arts curriculum. She exposed us to content in both the SAT and the ACT. She worked with the counselor's office to provide vouchers for students to take the examinations for free. We discussed the college admission process and identified focus strategies for our application. We made lists of target schools that fit within our reality. Ms. Hixson reviewed our lists to see whether we met the standards of the selected schools. She would often say, "Don't think you are applying to Harvard with a 1.9 GPA. Let us get realistic. You should have thought about that while you were playing."

We had to explain why we selected each school, how we thought it was a personal fit, what scholarships they offered that pertained to our interests and financing options. We wrote responses to sample college entry essay questions, which I hated because they required me to think outside of my comfort zone and disclose personal information.

Not only did we have to write on these deep topics, we also were required to dress up and present our responses (not reading verbatim). Ms. Hixson talked about the importance of effective communication, presentation skills, and looking professional. She told us, "No one will leave my classroom not knowing how to give an effective presentation. So, practice and remember that prior preparation prevents piss-poor performance." In addition to the résumé, we practiced effective interviewing skills for college and the workforce. Ms. Hixson encouraged us to attend college fairs, where we met and engaged with college representatives. She reminded us that admission officers initially learn about us from documents such as transcripts, ACT or SAT test scores, applications, essays, and recommendations. However, the interview would be our chance to talk positively about our interests, personalities, and other characteristics to boost our chance of admission.

Some of the questions that we had to answer were: "Describe in detail five important things about yourself"; "Tell me about your interests"; "Why do you want to attend our college?"; "What can you contribute?"; "What courses have you enjoyed most?"; "If you could change one thing about your high school, what would it be?"; "What is the most difficult situation you have faced?"; "What is your strongest/weakest point?"; "What have you done to prepare for college?"; "What has been your best experience in high school?"; "What are your biggest challenges?"; "Are your grades an accurate reflection of your potential?"; "Which of your activities is most rewarding and why?"; "What has been your biggest achievement?"; "What is your opinion on the presidential election process?"; "How did you spend last summer?"; "What do you want to do after you graduate from college?"; "What is your favorite book or author and why?"; and "What are you the proudest of?"

We were overwhelmed. However, we came to realize that her expectations and practices were preparing us for our future. She reminded us that although we were focusing on preparation and interviewing skills for college, the learning was transferrable to other situations in life. Ms. Hixson was breaking us down to build us up. She said, "Although many of you will be failing my class, please understand that you're more than just test scores or a grade." Despite all this encouragement, many of my classmates did not take academics seriously. Many of the other teachers did not demonstrate this level of commitment nor demand our attention. But I was grateful for these tips. No one had ever taken the time to explain how I should conduct myself in an interview for college or a job, or other situations in life.

While Ms. Hixson often talked about the interview process and reminded us that these skills are transferable, she also realized that college was not for everyone and everyone was not for college. In fact, it was quite clear that many students had no interest in attending college. Nevertheless, Ms. Hixson wanted to ensure that we were exposed to the possibilities that many of us had not even imagined. Also, she recognized that students needed preparation for their futures. She administered personality tests such as the Myers-Briggs Type Indicator, which is a psychological examination to determine how people perceive the world and make decisions. She helped us to identify potential career paths and occupations and to investigate each to determine the potential job growth, the starting salary, and what kind of work was involved. We had to explain the career trajectory for each position. As with the college interview process, she gave us tips on the job application process. Gloria Ladson-Billings (1994) coined the term *culturally relevant pedagogy* to describe "a pedagogy that empowers students intellectually, social, emotionally, and politically by using cultural referents to impart knowledge, skills, and attitudes" (p. 17). Similarly, Ms. Hixson consistently provided teaching strategies and pedagogy practices that were impactful to our future.

THE OPRAH CONNECTION

In my junior year, I was in a stage of transition. I had spent many years being bullied as a nerd, church boy, and mama's boy. I was searching for my identity. I was also in the process of shifting my personal appearance to fit in. I started trying to find swag, so I could be in the "in crowd." I worked to maintain at least a B average, so I could keep peace with my hard-working mom. I became more actively engaged and comfortable in making connections with peers in the inner circle. I was super busy on the JROTC Drill Team and percussion section leader of the marching band, playing the 30-inch Scotch bass drum. I was a part of the school chorus, the church choir, captain of the church step team, and president of the drama club. I did not prioritize thinking about college.

But from the day that I stayed to watch *Oprah* with Ms. Hixson, I began to make a connection with her. The episode that day told about how Oprah Winfrey had donated money to create an endowment of scholarships for Morehouse College. Ms. Hixson looked at me and said:

> You could be going to Morehouse, too, if you would start focusing on what you need to do and take this stuff serious. You are a rising senior and it is

> time to cut the bull crap. I need you to focus so you can be one of the young men that Oprah gives money to. You can be an Oprah Scholar. You can be a Morehouse Man!

Ms. Hixson cited the motto of the new president of Morehouse College, Dr. Robert Michael Franklin. She knew him personally as she was a member of his church. She told me about his formula for building the best Morehouse Man, whom he also called the Renaissance Man. She said that Dr. Franklin's concept was five wells: well read, well dressed, well spoken, well written, and well traveled. She described that being well read means to read books and develop versatile reading habits because books can enhance your knowledge and provide exposure. She described being well spoken as: "Good communication decreases the necessity of relying on profanity or empty vocal interrupters." Ms. Hixson noted that being well traveled allows people to see how various cultures strive and survive. She discussed the importance of being well dressed, which consisted of wearing appropriate attire in professional or social settings to demonstrate pride in appearance. Ms. Hixson reminded me that I had what it takes and that, if I focused, I could not only attend Morehouse, but I could thrive.

After the *Oprah* show ended, Ms. Hixson called Mr. Marshall Troup, a friend who worked in the counselor's office and oversaw a program called TRIO at Morehouse College. TRIO is a combination of outreach and student services programs designed to identify and provide services for individuals from disadvantaged backgrounds. Its mission was to assist low-income, first-generation college students and students with disabilities to progress through the academic pipeline from middle school to post-baccalaureate programs. After she made the introduction, I became a part of the TRIO Talent Search and Upward Bound programs. It changed my life and led to my decision to go to college. I went on multiple college tours and geared up for college. I completed the academic year and earned a B in Ms. Hixson's class.

As I entered my senior year, I was placed in Ms. Hixson's British literature course. She delivered the same approach, but I was now much more focused on preparation for college. After multiple college tours with the TRIO program, I decided that I wanted to attend Florida Agriculture and Mechanical University (FAMU), to major in teacher education. I also wanted to be part of the Marching 100. However, because I was now connected with Mr. Troup, who worked at Morehouse, he and Ms. Hixson highly recommended that I apply to Morehouse.

During the spring semester, I received a letter of denial from the college of my dreams, FAMU. I felt that I had wasted my time preparing to play in FAMU's band and would not become a Rattler and achieve the dream of being a college drum major. I became very depressed. However, 2 weeks later, I received a package of acceptance to Morehouse College.

While I did not understand how I had gained admittance to Morehouse College and not FAMU, I was grateful for Ms. Hixson. She had realized my potential, even when I did not realize my own potential and self-worth. She helped me to believe in myself, even when I did not. She did not judge me for my nerdiness, nor did she prejudge me because of the community where I came from. She provided tough love, high expectations, and a level of exposure outside of her students' comfort zones to help us to imagine the unimaginable.

Ladson-Billings (1994) posited the life-changing agenda of culturally relevant pedagogy is two-fold: It challenges traditional views of teaching and learning; and it develops a social consciousness among students in order to confront various forms of societal oppression. Likewise, Ms. Hixson taught us what it would be like to enter the real world. She reminded us that no one would feel sorry for us and that no one was required to give us anything. We would get where we wanted to go through tenacity, commitment, and hard work. She used her magic as an educator to leave me with what I often believe to be the Oprah Effect. Like Oprah, Ms. Hixson taught me the power of influence, the beauty of passion, the importance of being consistent, the importance of focus, the strength of being personal, a respect for uniqueness, the magic of inspiration, and the role of analytical thinking. I would learn later that both Ms. Hixson and Oprah had dreamed of becoming teachers. Perhaps new and future teachers could develop their own Oprah Effect to impact the lives of children like Ms. Hixson did for me.

RECOMMENDATIONS FOR PRESERVICE AND IN-SERVICE TEACHERS

The influences of Ms. Hixson on my current practice as an educator are many. However, I believe the following recommendations might be useful to current and future teachers:

1. *Educators should set the bar high for their students and provide rigorous and rewarding real-life experiences.* Every teacher should enter the classroom daily with *teacher effectiveness* and *high expectations* in mind. Their personal mission should be nothing less than to leave a direct imprint on the lives of their students, especially in an environment where excellence is not the norm. Students from these environments are often the victims of low expectations and poorly skilled teachers. Many never get exposed to teachers who hold them accountable and expose them to an education that strengthens them in multiple

domains. Teacher effectiveness and high expectations are important. Teachers must demonstrate professionalism and consistency, firmness, fairness, and friendliness, while setting high standards for achievement. Ms. Hixson was not always friendly, but her stern comments and quick wit, which were embedded in humor, allowed students to know that while she was human, she also had expectations that we would achieve to the best of our abilities.

2. *There should be a focus on intertwining the required academic content with "real-life" application.* This content should be taught in conjunction with developing students' professional skills. Students are more than academics and they will need skills to survive after high school. For example, teaching academic content in the context of communicating effectively across disciplines and domains helps a student learn an important skill that can be used for life.
3. *Use innovative strategies in teaching to promote learning.* Many students who come from under-resourced communities often do not know how to approach the learning environment. Ms. Hixson used multiple and unique methods and strategies to reach her students. For example, she used a speed dating setting to help us to be comfortable in talking about ourselves in a professional way. Teachers who fail to choose diverse ways of "reaching students" fail to understand the neurodiversity of the brain and may never assist students in learning how to contribute effectively to the classroom dynamic or integrate effectively in the larger society.
4. *Take time to build and create relationships with students.* The adage of "students don't care how much you know until they know how much you care" is still relevant for current and new teachers. The effective teacher takes time to connect with students individually and collectively. When I watched *Oprah* with Ms. Hixson, we connected. We communicated. We laughed. When she assigned the class written assignments, she allowed us to reveal important things about ourselves—our likes and dislikes, our successes and failures, our challenges. Ms. Hixson also understood how African American males are portrayed in the mass media and ensured that I knew that I was better than the media depictions, by teaching me that I could be resilient and defy the negative stereotypes portrayed in mass media.

CONCLUSION

The work of a teacher is challenging. However, the lesson learned from Ms. Hixson from her initial response, "It's 4 o'clock. I am off the clock, and it is time for me to watch *Oprah*. You should have done what you were supposed to do before now. You need to make an appointment. *Oprah* is on now. Bye!" has taught me the importance of setting standards and developing skills that students will need for life, whether that involves attending college or not. It was her demeanor, her actions, and her consistent commitment to me and my future that taught me how to push through and find the resilience that was within me to become the best human being I could be. Additionally, it was because of her touch and teachings that I learned I was not the African American male that the media often describe through a negative lens; however, I was the quite opposite and I had been equipped with the tools to defy mass media stereotypes. Teachers who choose to work with students in under-resourced communities should consider the magic of Ms. Hixson and create their own Oprah Effect to inspire students to rise above what they think they can achieve, and teach them that they too can find their resilience and defy negative mass media stereotypes.

REFERENCES

Adkins-Coleman, T. A. (2010). "I'm not afraid to come into your world": Case studies of teachers facilitating engagement in urban high school English classrooms. *Journal of Negro Education, 79*(1), 41–53.

Coakley, T. M. (2013). The influence of father involvement on child welfare permanency outcomes: A secondary data analysis. *Children and Youth Services Review, 35*(1), 174– 182.

Gipson, C. (2019). Delayed but NOT denied: How a Black male educational leader mastered resilience. In R. T. Palmer, M. O. Cadet, K. LeNiles, & J. L. Hughes (Eds.), *Personal narratives of Black educational leaders: Pathways to academic success* (pp. 111–121). New York, NY: Routledge.

Ladson-Billings, G. (1994). *The dreamkeepers: Successful teachers of African American students.* San Francisco, CA: Jossey-Bass.

Rapport, M. D., Bolden, J., Kofler, M. J., Sarver, D. E., Raiker, J. S., & Alderson, R. M. (2009). Hyperactivity in boys with attention-deficit/hyperactivity disorder (ADHD): A ubiquitous core symptom or manifestation of working memory deficits? *Journal of Abnormal Child Psychology, 37*(4), 521–534.

CHAPTER 5

ERNEST SMITH

Transforming Students Lives for 50 Years

Cleveland Hayes

You can't hoot with the owls at night and soar with the eagles the next morning.
—Ernest Smith

Distinguishing themselves professionally (Foster, 1995; Hayes & Juérez, 2012; Johnson, 2000), Black teachers have made significant contributions to the field of education in general and to the teaching of Black children in particular. Black teachers as a group and over time have consistently succeeded where others continue to fail at effectively teaching Black and other students often deemed hard to teach if not unteachable (Ladson-Billings, 1994, 1995; Lynn & Jennings, 2009).

Taken together, the successful approaches of Black teachers demonstrate that the persistent racial gaps in school discipline, educational opportunities, and attainment levels that continue to characterize U.S. public schooling are in no way natural or inevitable (Johnson, Boyden, & Pittz, 2001); these gaps persist because we as a nation allow them to do so. Black teachers' shared approaches to effective teaching for students historically underserved in classrooms provide a rich, albeit still mostly untapped, resource

The Impact of Classroom Practices, pages 41–53

for teacher educators and others vested in pushing against these persistent race-based educational disparities (Hayes & Juarez, 2012).

In education, there have always been Black men—Malcolm X, Carter G. Woodson, George Washington Carver, and W. E. B. Du Bois, to name just a few—who have refused to be defined and contained by an imperialist system of White supremacy, making use of every tool and means at their disposal to challenge and change that system and empower those targeted by it (hooks, 1992).

Importantly, the meager research that does exist on Black male teachers has examined the views of these educators about teaching in a variety of contexts and their reasons for entering the profession. In many cases, Black men have seen teaching as an opportunity to correct social, political, and even economic barriers to success for African Americans; they often have practiced a kind of critical race praxis that is aimed at ending racial inequality and challenging White supremacy (Hayes, 2006; Lynn, 2004, 2006a, 2006b; Lynn & Jennings, 2009).

Because their daily lives, and therefore the stories they tell about their work, reflect the influence of and their engagement with the imperialist system of White racial domination. The viewpoints of Black men provide a significant yet still largely untapped resource. As an education community we can use these strategies coupled with a viable research base to better support and nurture academic success among African American and other students of color. I ask, following Richard Wright (1957), "Is it not clear to you that the American Negro is the only group in our nation that consistently and passionately raises the question of freedom? This is a service to America and the world" (p. 101).

The purpose of this chapter is to explore the philosophies of one Black male teacher who impacted the lives of students in one community for 50 years, Mr. Ernest Smith, in hopes of providing a valuable source of knowledge on effective schooling. I hope that we can glean from this what it means to be a successful educator not only for Black students but for all students within a societal context constantly changing (King, 1993; Lynn & Jennings, 2009; Ware, 2002).

LEARNING FROM THE NARRATIVE OF MR. SMITH: MY PURPOSE OF INQUIRY

In this chapter, I introduce Mr. Ernest Smith, respectfully known for his effectiveness in teaching Black and other students typically deemed unteachable, from the American South. He attended and taught in public schools during and immediately following the integration of classrooms albeit nearly two decades after the passage of the landmark 1954 Supreme

Court ruling of the *Brown v. Board of Education* decision declaring the "separate but equal" dictum unconstitutional and having no place in public schooling. This chapter draws on critical race theory (CRT) and its emphasis on the value and usefulness of subjugated people's lived experiences and knowledge in exposing processes of racial domination to highlight and examine the silence in the literature on Black male teachers, in particular, and the successful teaching of African American students in general by examining the perspectives and theorizing of these three African American men regarding their work and lives as an educator.

Pointedly, students of color are the coming coming—and in some places, already established—*diverse new majority* in U.S. public schools (Hayes, 2014). Students of color, Black and Latino students, in particular, are also more likely to go to prison than to college (Noguera, 2003, 2008; Wacquant, 2001). At the same time, as Joyce King (2005) has observed, "The abysmal state of Black education in the United States and globally is an inhumane situation that calls into question the values and pronouncements of Western civilization" (p. 3). For the promise of *Brown* to be realized and this pernicious school-to-prison pipeline to be interrupted, then, all of us—teachers, teacher educators, and others vested in democratic principles and outcomes in education—must learn what these and other Black educators have long known—that is to say, how to teach *all* students effectively. As Lynn (Lynn, Johnson, & Hassan, 1999) has observed, "[V]ery few studies have explored how African American men who teach in emancipator ways view their teaching" (p. 43). Drawing from the viewpoints and pedagogies of Black male educators who are successful teachers of African American students and other students of color, this chapter both extends the literature on the lives and work of Black teachers and attempts to help push forward and move beyond existing understandings of culturally relevant forms of teaching and learning by linking the practice of teaching and everyday life to the political, while using knowledge developed through struggle within and against the historical context of White supremacy.

HOW TO READ THIS CHAPTER

Like the teachers in Foster's (1995) study, the educator presented in this chapter was identified and chosen through direct contact with the African American community. Mr. Smith, also similar to the teachers in Foster's study, is considered and known within his school, neighborhood, and personal and professional communities as a highly successful teacher in terms of his effectiveness in teaching and working with predominantly Black student populations.

Pointedly, and this is very significant, I must caution against reading the narrative presented in this chapter as a recipe cookbook, a how-to-guide or any other kind of (re)source of magic-bullet formulas on how to successfully teach Black and other racial minoritized students and thus "fix" our schools. There will be no recipes provided herein through the narrative or otherwise. As I define them, teaching and learning are cultural work, ways of thinking and thus approaching life and its many domains, including education. It is not a technocratic, rational, objective, and mechanistic process or procedure. Moreover, in education, we already have a plethora of narrowly defined curricula, that is to say, scripted pedagogies and standardized assessments that are proven failures despite the good intentions from which they were developed (Hayes, 2014; Quijada Cercer, Alvarez, & Rios, 2010).

I take the stance that teaching is not a "what to do" endeavor, but rather a "how to think" one because, following Ladson-Billings (2006) and this narrative, while the educator in this study believed that students deserve a demanding curriculum, he was also not necessarily attached to any specific teaching strategy or curricular program. Mr. Smith viewed his mission and role in education in a particular way that is based on using his teaching to ensure the survival and well-being of all Black children. Because this teacher thinks about his students in ways that are not dependent on assumptions of Black cultural and moral deficiencies and assumptions of White moral and cultural superiority, the teaching approaches he used likewise was not aimed as compensating for the (supposed) cultural and moral deficiencies of Black children and guiding Black students toward acceptance of and assimilation into the existing system of White supremacy.

In this chapter, I am concerned with a particular Black male teacher who taught during and immediately after the Jim Crow era of racial apartheid in the American South. I aim to highlight the pedagogical practices and philosophies of Mr. Smith as a way to show how he drew on his lived cultural and gendered knowledge and experiences to successfully teach African Americans. What we will see as a theme in Mr. Smith's narrative are the struggles of this teacher as he attempted to use his teaching as a means to end racial inequality by challenging the historically embedded notion of Black inferiority (O'Connor, 2006)—a set of beliefs widely held among Whites suggesting that, for example, African Americans tend to be unmotivated, less intelligent, and more aggressive and violent than Whites, that African Americans prefer welfare over working for a living and have poor parenting skills, and that African Americans have an overall less sophisticated and well-developed culture and morality than Whites (Feagin, Vera, & Batur, 2001; Picca & Feagin, 2007). By default, importantly, assumptions of Black cultural and moral inferiority necessarily imply assumptions of White cultural and moral superiority.

I hope readers will recognize how Mr. Smith saw his teaching as a moral obligation to help his students learn to challenge and work toward eliminating social inequalities and institutional oppression in pursuit of a more robust democracy. With many pressing issues in education, I hope readers will learn from the narrative presented in this chapter by taking the experience and perspective shared by Mr. Smith and use it as a call to act against inequities in education and society and thus, like him, become agents of change and school culture shifters (Hayes, 2014; Dixson & Rousseau, 2005; Freire, 1973; Lynn, 2006a; Quijada Cercer et al., 2010; Yosso, 2005).

YOU CAN'T PARTAKE OF THE FIFTH ON THE FOURTH AND EXPECT TO COME FOURTH ON THE FIFTH
Mr. Ernest Smith

"Before there was STEM (science, technology, engineering, and math) for girls, there was Mr. Smith," Henderson shared. "He encouraged many and influenced a lot of us to be who we are today" (Brown, 2015).

"He was the kind of person who would help anyone," Edwards shared. "His classes collected canned food items during the holidays for LOVE's Kitchen and never wanted the prize given to the class that collected the most" (Brown, 2015).

"You're gonna f-f-fail by getting a f-f-freddy frog," for an F grade and "Stop drinkin' that wiinne, and you might be on tiiime!" to anyone late to his class, but managed to make it through the door before he locked it (Brown, 2015).

As an educator for more than 50 years, Smith retired from MPSD in August 2009. A native of Starkville, he attended Oktibbeha County Training School and finished number one in his senior class. Two days after graduating from high school, Smith was inducted into the U.S. Army. After 6 years, Smith enrolled at Jackson State College, where he received a Bachelor of Science degree. He also earned a master's degree in physical science. After Mr. Smith passed, the Meridian Star, the local newspaper, ran a special feature article about the legacy of Mr. Smith as a teacher in the Meridian Public Schools. The quotations in italics are what his former students said about him as a teacher and the impact he had on the community for some 50 years. Mr. Smith was one of a kind, and there is a void where he once occupied time and space.

When Mr. Smith began his public school education career, first as a student and then as a teacher, this need for learning which prepares African American youth for freedom, respectability, and self-reliance had not changed. As a student, Mr. Smith was taught by his teachers that he must be prepared for freedom, respectability, and self-reliance. Then as a teacher, in turn, Mr. Smith taught his students that they too must be prepared for freedom, respectability, and self-reliance.

In the following paragraphs, I present the narrative of Mr. Smith and how he approached his work as a teacher serving a predominantly Black community. His narrative is based upon the main ideas that emerged from his description of his approaches to teaching and learning. I begin Mr. Smith's story by explaining how he understands the role and significance of education and, then, how he implements his views on education and their importance in his teaching practices.

MR. SMITH: I TEACH NOT ONLY THE COURSE, BUT I ALSO TEACH LIFE

I teach because I know I'm helping many kids. Plus, I like what I do. And anytime you're on a job, and you like what you do, you do a better job. My kids are learning and I've seen the results of the kids going out and doing well.

I have taken the experiences from my own teachers to create this environment in my class that is respected by the students, the parents, and the community. We need to know where we came from, and we never need to forget where we came from. We need to know and have the ability to guide all of the kids that we teach, regardless of race, in the right direction.

I have one philosophy. I try and explain my expectations to my students: If you plan to pass this course, you must study every day, as if you were having a test the next day. This is not a course that you can stay up all night and cram and get ready to pass the test. It won't happen, but if you do a little studying every day with all of your courses, with spending more time with the most difficult, the less time with the less difficult, then you'll do well in school.

I believe that all kids can learn. I believe that I have to do something to make them learn, or to help them learn—whether it is patting them on the back, or kicking them in the butt, begging them, or demanding. I have to figure out every student and do the best I can to get the best I can from them. I instill in them the importance of an education if one wishes to be successful. I instill in them that they should be better than their parents—they should surpass their parents. I instill in them that they must be honest and do the very best they can all of the time. I instill in them to be kind and to respect each other. They have to speak to each other and speak to me with respect. I try my best to not only teach the course that I teach, but I also teach life experiences that they need to know about. And I do this from Day 1.

There are a couple of things that I think frame my way of thinking about education that can be passed on to the next generation of teachers. First, in my community the most important man, or the most important person, after the home, was the preacher. The next most important and respected person was the teacher. They were very much so respected.

All of the men were called professors, even though they might not have had a BS degree and most of them didn't. They were called professors. And now some of the older teachers, the older Black teachers that worked with me, we called each other professor, or just 'fessor, after a matter of respect for our heritage. It's not that we are professors because we don't teach at a college, and we don't have a professorship, and we don't get paid what professors get paid, but it's a matter of carrying over our heritage and respect for our people before us.

Second, I enjoy it. I enjoy taking students where they are and bringing them to where they should have been and carrying them to where I want them to be. I enjoy seeing them come out successful.

We, as teachers, regardless of race, I think that you are going to prepare yourself to overcome the many obstacles that you will encounter. I think that you should not only be a person who is a leader but a person whom other people will follow, as well. Other people, meaning not only your students but also your peers, in your profession and your community. I think that you should never give up on any student. I think you have to do your best all the time for your students.

Mr. Smith's love of teaching and students, importantly, emerges forcefully from his narrative—he teaches because he loves working with students. That love of students and teaching is communicated to his students and their families and then reciprocated. This love of students and teaching is not the interpersonal, individual, psychological feeling that Dr. Martin Luther King, Jr. termed "emotional bosh" typically associated with this word (Cone, 2004, p. 130). It is instead a reference to respect in its robust form of putting a positive value on the students and the communities and families they come from and the cultural experiences and knowledge they bring with them. We experienced this mutual respect in all of our interactions with Mr. Smith and when we crossed those boundaries we experienced his warm demanding. Mr. Smith positively valued his students and the communities they represent by likewise emphasizing through and in his teaching the importance of and *need to know where we came from.* Mr. Smith's emphasis on the importance of education in the Black community historically as well as his explanation of how he and other Black teachers referred to each other as "'fessor" are useful illustrations of how the connection and respect for the cultural heritage and background of the students are incorporated into his approach to teaching and daily practices. Mr. Smith expected his students to understand that this valuing of education was part of their cultural heritage and thus belonged in his teaching and in the classroom as part of the curriculum.

There was a historical aspect to Mr. Smith's teaching. By understanding and bringing into his teaching the historical experiences and accomplishments of the Black community, Mr. Smith used and applied discernment in his teaching. This positive valuing of the Black community in his teaching practices and approach is notable because it is most often the case that African Americans and their cultural backgrounds are typically represented often as pathological aberrations of dominant White society's cultural forms and therefore of no use or value in the classroom (Foster, 1997).

Pointedly, students were in the center of Mr. Smith's talk about his teaching approach and practices. Mr. Smith, departing from conventional notions and pedagogies of teaching and learning, did not expect students to conform to him; and find ways to connect with him, rather, he works to conform to them and find a way to connect with them using a range of strategies—from patting them on the back to demanding their cooperation. Put simply, Mr. Smith, as their teacher, took on the responsibility of his students' learning. Unlike traditional forms of teaching and learning, which put the locus of responsibility on the child, Mr. Smith saw it as his purpose as a teacher to reach his students and make connections with them as the first step in helping them to be successful in school. If students are not learning, Mr. Smith saw this as a reflection of himself as a teacher, not a failure on the part of the students.

Mr. Smith did not draw on or default to deficiency notions of Black students and their cultural background to explain the challenges they face in the classroom. His willingness to take ownership and responsibility for their learning suggests that he saw himself as invested in his students' learning and did not draw on understandings of Black inferiority to avoid taking responsibility for his students' learning. As Mr. Smith put it, "You has to do your best all the time for your students." This need to *do your best all the time for your students* locates the locus of responsibility in the teacher as the professional educator in charge of the classroom and students' learning.

By taking responsibility for students' learning on himself as a professional educator and then making connections to students, Mr. Smith set the stage in his classroom to foster his students' successful learning. At the same time, Mr. Smith saw the curriculum as more than academic content in his class. More specifically, students were not merely learning academic content for the sake of learning academic content. For Mr. Smith, success in school required academic learning as a stepping stone or basis for being successful in living and life in general. As Mr. Smith explained, "I try my best to not only teach the course that I teach, but I also teach life experiences that they need to know about."

For Mr. Smith, curricular content was thus tied to life and being successful in life. He views teaching as more than simply conveying academic facts and bits of knowledge. This expanded view of teaching as more than transmitting knowledge is critical because it underscores the contextual and historical aspects of Mr. Smith's teaching approach and practices. Mr. Smith also sought to use his teaching as a means to advocate for Black children.

He focused his work as a teacher on making connections with students and helping them to view themselves and their efforts in school as part of a much bigger and historical endeavor to improve the social conditions of the Black community and Black children in particular.

CLOSING OUT: THEORIZING THE THEORY

In today's educational parlance, we are always talking about these "hard to teach" kids as if that task is so very impossible. Yet, there have always been those in the Black community who have made a way out of no way. As Ladson-Billings (1994) has repeatedly argued, the contemporary education community needs to look to those who have accomplished this feat for the wisdom, knowledge, and strategies about how we too might do what previously seemed an impossible task. I hope that the narrative of Mr. Smith shared in this study will assist educators, policymakers, and vested others in better understanding the social justice-oriented teaching approaches that African American teachers have historically employed to foster the academic success of Black students and to offer a vision of a more socially just society. Until we take it upon ourselves to follow teachers like Mr. Smith in viewing the world through a lens that is grounded in an anti-racist struggle and which does not affirm assumptions of Black inferiority and White superiority, our recipe-like practices and what-to-do approaches will continue in the already deeply entrenched and well-trodden path of White supremacy predictably proving futile in our public schools. At the same time, the dream of equal education for all students remains yet elusive.

At the heart of CRT is an appreciation for storytelling. Following hooks (1992), the narrated story of Mr. Smith presented in this chapter is essential because his existence functions to counter the institutionalized ignorance of Black history and culture as well as Blacks' existence not only in education but in the broader national and global historical context. The field of education needs successful counter-stories and testimonies of Black educators who worked within education in the past to help us to understand how we in the present might successfully prepare African American students in today's racially charged society. It is the stories of oppression and resistance of the past that we can use as a framework for better understanding and navigating the present within the historical context of White supremacy (Lynn, 2004).

The application of CRT in this chapter allowed me to focus on the voice of teachers like Mr. Smith to learn more about how to think about and use teaching as a form of cultural work to successfully teach African American students and realize a transformative education for all. By successfully teaching African American students, Mr. Smith worked to challenge the dominance of White superiority. The use of CRT makes it possible for me to tap into the knowledge and understandings that he used to effectively teach African American students and hope to accomplish half of what Mr. Smith did across several decades.

RECOMMENDATIONS FOR PRACTICE: WHAT CAN WE LEARN FROM MR. SMITH

If there is one take-away from this section, according to Ware (2006), culturally and politically responsive teachers teach with authority, a form of teaching that includes teaching to the whole child as a member of a particular social group situated within a particular context and history. However, being a warm demander is more than coming into the classroom and demanding a checklist of certain behaviors from students. Effective teaching of African American students is not about implementing a particular step-by-step remedy plan. Black and Latino kids, for example, see White teachers arrive in their communities stand up before them, attempting to teach them a curriculum that is already pre-determined and defined in terms of what they need to know. Consequently, the students can in turn answer questions on a standardized test that are likely to have little to no bearing on their actual lived experiences and realities. The teachers, in turn, do not have any connection to their students and neither does the curriculum they are attempting to teach (Juarez & Hayes, 2012; Hayes & Juarez, 2012).

Teachers cannot be warm demanders by doing drive-by teaching. Teachers must be invested in, deeply familiar with, and able to find and draw on the richness and beauty of the communities in which they teach. Teachers must not go into communities with the mentality to save the students from themselves, their parents, their culture, or their history and thus miss the resiliency, richness, and beauty of the ways groups and individuals have learned to cope and thrive within a historical context of near-constant race-based hostility and forms of nonaggressions, sabotage, and assault perpetrated by the dominant society.

The paradox of teacher preparation, however, is that most teachers, teacher educators, and future teachers are White. Teacher education in the United States is a White world (Hayes & Juarez, 2009). Most White people have developed very little familiarity with or investments in African American or any other racial minority community in the United States.

What can a predominantly White field of educators learn from Mr. Smith? Mr. Smith as an African American male, logically, is more than likely to have the familiarity with and investments in the African American community required for the effectively teaching of African American learners.

Do teachers thus have to be Black to learn from Mr. Smith's lessons? Since White people and others from outside of the African American community tend not to have these same connections and familiarity, are they necessarily excluded from the pool of potentially effective teachers of African American learners? I posit that the answer is a resounding "No!"

First, race is a social construction. People must therefore learn their racial identities. While the realities of race and racism are very real and historically embedded, they are not biologically determined. Accordingly, there is no inherent biological or other natural barrier to keep White and other non-Black people from learning from Mr. Smith (Juarez & Hayes, 2012; Hayes & Juarez, 2012).

Second, and accordingly, Mr. Smith's lessons constitute an approach to teaching and learning, not a step-by-step formula or recipe. He viewed his work as teacher from a particular perspective that includes an awareness of and an activism against White racism. His lessons explicitly are aware of, know about, and work against assumptions of Black inferiority and White superiority. Hence, Mr. Smith's lessons are perspectives and ways of thinking about and making sense of the world that can be learned and adopted by anyone regardless of background (Juarez & Hayes, 2012; Hayes & Juarez, 2012).

Moreover, because Mr. Smith's lessons are not technical step-by-step formulas, they cannot be mechanically implemented as a type of technocratic, objective, rational process. To learn from Big Mama's recipes requires us to understand and interpret them within the context from which they were derived and developed. In particular, Mr. Smith's lessons require us to develop an awareness of the historical and group context, not the individual as an entity outside of group membership and history.

The focus of Smiths's lessons is not simply on the cognitive and psychological well-being of students, but incorporates an awareness of and challenge to the ways White racism negatively influences the individual's psychological, social, and other forms of well-being. In other words, Mr. Smith affirmed the contributions and validity of Black culture, experiences, and history. He did not view his Black students or the surrounding community as a deficient and corrupt version of European American culture.

Without an awareness of history and context infused into teaching approaches and practices, Mr. Smith's lessons are likely to become just another set of prescriptive recipes that fall by the wayside in schools. To learn from Mr. Smith, we must learn to identify and work against the consequences of White racism that influence students of color and privilege students who benefit from the systemic privileging of Whiteness presently and historically within U.S. society. We too must familiarize ourselves with the gifts of Black folks and develop a vested interest in communities of color an investment not based on the patronizing and ultimately harmful effects of presuming Whiteness as the normative standard.

REFERENCES

Brown, I. (2015). *Smith remembered by former students.* Retrieved from http://m.meridianstar.com/news/smith-remembered-by-former-students/article_f805d3ce-a47e-11e5-ba1b-6fd8f0ca23c2.html?mode=jqm

Cone, J. H. (2004). *Martin and Malcolm and America: A dream or a nightmare.* Maryknoll, NY: Orbis Books.

Dixson, A. D., & Rousseau, C. K. (2005). And we are still not saved: Critical race theory in education ten years later. *Race, Ethnicity, and Education, 8*(1), 7–27.

Feagin, J., Vera, H., & Batur, P. (2001). *White racism: The basics* (2nd ed.). New York, NY: Routledge.

Freire, P. (1973). *Pedagogy of the oppressed.* New York, NY: Continuum.

Foster, M. (1995). African American teachers and culturally relevant pedagogy. In J. Banks & C. M. Banks (Eds.), *Handbook of research on multicultural education* (pp. 570–581). New York, NY: Macmillan.

Foster, M. (1997). *Black teachers on teaching.* New York, NY: The New Press.

Hayes, C. (2006). *Why we teach: Storytelling the lives of Black family of Mississippi educators.* Unpublished doctoral dissertation, University of Utah, Salt Lake City.

Hayes, C. (2014). We teach too: What are the lived experiences and pedagogical practices of gay men or color teachers? *Masculinities and Social Change, 3*(2), 148–172.

Hayes, C., & Juarez, B. G. (2012). There is no culturally responsive teaching spoken here: A critical race perspective. *Democracy and Education, 20*(1), article 1.

hooks, b. (1992). *Black looks: Race and representation.* Boston, MA: South End Press.

Juárez, B. G., & Hayes, C. (2012). An embarked learning and transformative education for freedom dreams: The education our children deserve. *Journal of Education Controversy, 6*(1).

Johnson, K. A. (2000). *Uplifting the women and the race: The lives and educational philosophies and social activism of Anna Julia Cooper and Nannie Helen Burroughs.* New York, NY: Routledge.

Johnson, T., Boyden, J. E., & Pittz, W. (Eds.). (2001). *Racial profiling and punishment in U.S. public schools: How zero tolerance policies and high stakes testing subvert academic excellence and racial equity.* Oakland, CA: Applied Research Center.

King, J. (2005). *Black education: A transformative research and action agenda for the new century.* New York, NY: Routledge.

King, S. H. (1993). The limited presence of African American teachers. *Review of Educational Research, 63*(2), 115–149.

Ladson-Billings, G. (1994). *The dreamkeepers: Successful teachers of African American children.* San Francisco, CA: Jossey-Bass.

Ladson-Billings, G. (1995). Toward a theory of culturally relevant pedagogy. *American Educational Research Journal, 32*(3), 465–491.

Ladson-Billings, G. (2006). Yes, but how do we do it? In J. Landsman & C. W. Lewis (Eds.), *White teachers, diverse classrooms* (pp. 29–42). Sterling, VA: Stylus.

Lynn, M. (2004). Inserting the "race" into critical pedagogy: An analysis of "race-based epistemologies." *Educational Philosophy and Theory, 36*(2), 153–165.

Lynn, M. (2006a). Dancing between two worlds: A portrait of the life of a Black male teacher in South Central LA. *International Journal of Qualitative Studies in Education, 19*(2), 221–242.

Lynn, M. (2006b). Education for the community: Exploring the culturally relevant practices of Black male teachers. *Teachers College Record, 108*(12), 2497–2522.

Lynn, M., & Jennings, M. E. (2009). Power, politics, and critical race theory: A critical race analysis of Black male teachers' pedagogy. *Race Ethnicity and Education, 12*(2), 173–196.

Noguera, P. A. (2003). Schools, prisons, and social implications of punishment: Rethinking disciplinary practices. *Theory into Practice, 42*(4), 341–350.

Noguera, P. A. (2008). *The trouble with Black boys and other reflections on race, equity, and the future of public education.* San Francisco, CA: Jossey-Bass.

O'Connor, C. (2006). The premise of Black inferiority: An enduring obstacle fifty years post-*Brown.* In A. Ball (Ed.), *With more deliberate speed: Achieving equity and excellence in education—Realizing the full potential of Brown v. Board of Education* (pp. 316–336). New York, NY: Teachers College Press.

Picca, L. H., & Feagin, J. R. (2007). *Two-faced racism: Whites in the backstage and frontstage.* New York, NY: Routledge.

Quijada Cerecer, P. D., Gutiérrez Alvarez, L., & Rios, F. (2010). Critical multiculturalism: Transformative educational principles and practices. In T. K. Chapman & N. Hobbel (Eds.), *Social justice pedagogy across the curriculum: The practice of freedom* (pp. 144–163). New York, NY: Routledge.

Wacquant, L. (2001). Deadly symbiosis: When ghetto and prison meet and mesh. *Punishment and Society, 3*(1), 95–133.

Ware, F. (2002). Black teachers' perceptions of their professional roles and practices. In J. J. Irvine (Ed.), *In search of wholeness: African American teachers and their culturally specific classroom practices* (pp. 33–46). New York, NY: Palgrave.

Ware, F. (2006). Warm demander pedagogy: Culturally responsive teaching that supports a culture of achievement for African American students. *Urban Education, 41*(4), 427–456.

Wright, R. (1957). *White man, listen!* Berkeley, CA: HarperPerennial.

Yosso, T. (2005). Whose culture has capital? A critical race theory discussion on community cultural wealth. *Race Ethnicity and Education, 8*(1), 69–61.

CHAPTER 6

I AM BECAUSE YOU ARE

The Importance of Being Given Roots to Grow and Wings to Fly

Tiffany Hollis

There are only two lasting bequests we can hope to give our children. One of these is roots, the other wings. Good parents give their children roots and wings: roots to know where home is, and wings to fly off and practice what has been taught to them.

—Jonas Salk

I had heard the above saying before, but I recently heard this while in conversation with a fellow colleague: "Wings show you what you can become, while roots remind you of where you are from." There were many people and situations that helped me to soar and rise above the risks and adverse situations that I faced. There were times when my wings were clipped and needed to be mended; however, once they were mended, my flight towards my destiny continued. I am reminded daily of where I am from, especially by those who might not have "made it" or who may not be happy with their current situations. Growing up in Gaffney, South Carolina did not allow for much exposure to positive examples of women of color who were successful. I am what some might call "the exception." I do not know of many

The Impact of Classroom Practices, pages 55–64

young women who grew up in similar situations like me to have attained a doctorate degree. Although my story is still being written, it is my hope that this account of my journey proves that despite challenges and complexities, one's fate is not sealed and he or she can overcome adversity and live a productive life.

I am currently a tenure-track assistant professor at a Predominantly White Liberal Arts Institution in South Carolina. I have my PhD in curriculum and instruction (urban education) from UNC Charlotte. I received my BA in history and a minor in secondary education from Davidson College in Davidson, NC before attaining a Master's in education from Columbia College in Columbia, SC and a graduate certificate in teaching in special education from UNC Charlotte. According to my family history, my neighborhood, and the circumstances in which I grew up, I am not supposed to have made it this far. I am a living witness that starting life with disadvantages does not mean that one's destiny is defined. Many never leave Gaffney or venture out of their comfort zone. I, on the other hand, saw what staying in Gaffney could do to a person's psyche and I decided I wanted to break the cycle and move out of the area. I was determined to prove those who had doubted my ability to be successful wrong, while making a better life for me beyond the life and circumstances that I was forced to grow up in.

As a young African American girl, I grew up in adverse childhood situations, experienced chronic poverty, lived in a single-parent household with my mother. I was faced with numerous obstacles, but managed to defy stereotypes held of children who grow up in poverty similar to me. How was I able to remain strong and resilient? Who helped me to rise above harsh and unyielding obstacles? What factors within the context of my journey, positive and negative, helped me to succeed in spite of adverse circumstances? I began to develop a mindset to "expect greater." I had some help from my mentor whom I will speak about later in the chapter.

WHAT DOES IT MEAN TO EXPECT GREATER?

Expecting greater means to be able to develop resilience and survive and even thrive in the face of difficulty. Expecting greater is the ability of a person to adapt, so that he or she can triumph over obstacles. As we face difficulties, our resilience alters to meet and overcome new challenges, and consequently, we expect greater. Oftentimes having a mentor and a strong relationship with a caring and supportive adult in the classroom or in the education setting helps one to expect greater of oneself.

CHALLENGES MAKE YOU STRONGER

The saying "How you start is not how you end up" emphasizes that despite challenges and complexities that may be faced, one's fate is not sealed and he or she can overcome adversity and live a productive life. Consequently, youth who have been labeled as "at-risk" in terms of societal definitions can use the protective factors in their lives to transform into "at-opportunity" and become productive citizens who contribute to society (Hollis & Goings, 2017, p. 888). According to the history of my family, I am not supposed to have attained the level of education that I have attained thus far. Starting life with disadvantages does not mean that one's destiny is defined. I was born into a family where my mother dropped out of high school and by the age of 21, she already had two children out of wedlock by two fathers. My mother worked hard to provide for her children and even lived with her mother so that she could try to get on her feet as a young single mother who had limited education. We eventually moved to South Carolina to live with my great-grandmother, who we affectionately called Big Mama. My mother made a decision to move out of the house with my great-grandmother and show and prove that she could make it without support from her mother and my great grandmother.

Although my mother worked hard, we still were faced with times where the hot water was turned off, food was uncertain, and it was a constant struggle to provide even the most basic of needs. Like others born into generational poverty, I eventually realized that my educational journey was born out of necessity—a necessity to move out of poverty—and education seemed to be my vehicle. I also knew that I had obstacles in my path such as memories of violence from the sporadic, yet rampant incidents of domestic violence that my mother experienced, emotional un-attachment of my mother (not because she did not love me, but because she was dealing with some of her own issues at times), not knowing my father, and just sheer fear of not knowing what was going to happen next in a place that was supposed to be "home" and provide a nurturing and caring environment. School became a safe space for me, but it also became a place where I felt invisible. Not many people paid attention to the young African American girl with an attitude and a smart mouth, who would fight anyone (including teachers) if they even looked at her the wrong way or made an ignorant comment. In fact, many teachers just wanted me out of their classrooms, so the referrals and the suspensions added up. I would get suspended from school only to engage in some risky behaviors in the neighborhood in which I lived. My mother worked several jobs and oftentimes she was unaware of the things that I was doing.

No one at the schools talked to me to find out why my behavior had abruptly changed and why I was starting to get into so much trouble. From that point forward, I got into fights daily that eventually became physical. I talked back to the teachers and even made threats towards my teachers. Little did they know that I was crying out for help as the situation at home was getting worse and I began to lose focus and get into more and more arguments and fights, which led to more suspensions. I would miss school and come back and ace the tests and even be prepared for the next lesson because I had read ahead in my "spare time."

The fights, defiance, and disrespect continued well into middle school. It was as if my reputation preceded me because I had teachers who would write me off before I could even open my mouth in their classrooms. I had been labeled as the bad girl who was a class clown and who had a mouth on her. I had a few teachers who tried to challenge me and then I had some who actually cared about me. There was no such thing as gifted and talented in the middle school. Instead, you were placed on a track to be in the college prep track or the regular track. Even though my behavior was atrocious, I made straight "A" honor roll, which confused so many of the teachers with whom I interacted. It soon became evident that I was smart, but I was a combination of being book smart and street smart. This was a combination that many adults had no clue how to handle. As a result of being that smart Black girl, I became the only minority student in many of my classes over the years. In order to be successful, I had to conform to the dominant standards and start to embrace this "new" identity to which I was slowly adapting. For me, there was opposition each school year as the inner conflict continued as I struggled with being the honor student I *had become* and the stereotypical student on welfare growing up without a father that others *expected me to be* when I returned to my neighborhood each day.

The next few years, I struggled with trying to find out where I fit in as I juggled my workload at school, the issues at home, helping my mother with adult responsibilities at home, and even trying to still be that "hard" girl who did not take any mess. I was looking for a support system and crying out for help and it seemed as if no one heard me. I felt as if my wings had been clipped and I was left to venture on this journey without much support. Where were my roots and my wings during this difficult transition in my life?

Research shows that the presence of just one caring adult in the life of a child can make a difference between success and failure in school (Gay, 2000). It was in middle school that I met my mentor, who was also my guidance counselor. Dr. Dorse Cleveland, as I affectionately called her, pulled me out to talk with me one day. She said that she had noticed that I was getting into a lot of trouble, so she asked me if I wanted to talk to her. I told her that I did not know her like that and she should mind her business. She called me to her office the next day and offered to share a positive quote with me. She gave me several quotes and she would ask me if I tried journaling and getting things out that way. I went to her office a few times a week to write, read, eat, and just listen to her talk. I did not say much at first and then I told her to just give up. She told me that I was used to everyone giving up on me and that she was not going to give up on me or go anywhere because she saw potential in me. She told me that I was destined for greatness. She reminded me that as long as I embraced who I was and whose I was that I could achieve anything despite my shortcomings. At first, it was hard for her to break down the barrier that I had put up. Understanding protective factors that foster resilience and increase school connectedness is crucial to helping children who have experienced violence in their urban neighborhoods and are chronically exposed to violence (Hollis, 2019). I refer to her being able to reach me and to foster a sense of connection with me by using a model that I have coined as the "CARE model" of teaching. However; in this case, I am attributing it to the role of guidance counselors as teachers (Hollis & Goings, 2017).

Consequently, the CARE model explores the role that (C) culturally relevant pedagogy, (A) attachment to school, (R) regulating emotions (mental health), and (E) expectations of teachers play in narrowing or closing the gaps (Hollis & Goings, 2017). This multifaceted approach is essential to meet the needs of youth who are frequently underserved, and often profoundly "left behind," by the educational system. Although she was a guidance counselor, I learned so much from Dr. Dorse Cleveland in terms of being educated and not just schooled. She would talk to me about so many things and just speak positivity into my life even though I continued to pretend as if I was not listening. Thus, I use this model to speak to how although she was not an educator in the classroom, she educated me beyond the confinement of a classroom and played a vital role in why I am who I am and why I am where I am today.

She placed me in numerous activities after school and would take me home so that I could not give her the excuse that I did not have a ride. She placed me in several events, activities, and even summer programs that would help me nurture that potential that she said she had noticed in me. She even began to teach me how to talk to adults in a more respectful manner, how to turn my anger into something positive, and how to honor and respect my mother and the decisions that she made because she was still my mother, despite the issues and decisions that she made. I felt as if my wings had been mended and I felt invincible. She took the time and energy to make me feel as if I mattered, as if my life mattered despite my past circumstances. Over the years, my trajectory started to change and I began to move in the right direction in life. She stayed right by my side the entire time and fostered a sense of resilience. According to Masten (1999), resilience usually refers to positive results in spite of threats. Before continuing my narrative, I need to place the term resilience in a social context. According to Benard (2004), resilience denotes the process, the ability to bounce back from stressors, challenges, and trials. For the purposes of this chapter, resilience will be viewed as the developmental process that improves people as they adapt to adversity in order to triumph (Hollis, 2016). Her actions were similar to those that were modeled by the teachers who Ladson-Billings (2009) called "Dreamkeepers" who, as noted in her book, were like coaches, believing students were capable of excellence.

My mentor was integral in my life after our initial meeting in middle school as I started to slowly transform and become a better person. She gave me information about college preparatory programs, nominated me for awards, and often would register me for various contests and opportunities. She took a vested interest in me and certainly helped me to channel my anger into something positive. I remember when she strategically had me placed at an internship with her through a program called YOU (Youth Opportunities Unlimited) at Limestone College in Gaffney, where I had a job over the summer and was given a stipend. Being at the school with her and the principal, Dr. Carol McFadden, who was also an African American female allowed me to see firsthand how schools operated. Consequently, it also gave her a chance to keep me under her supervision and away from my boyfriend who was 18 at the time and a drug dealer. She knew I had been sneaking around to see him and spending more time with him than I should have been at my age. She did not judge or condescend my decisions. Instead, she continued to affirm that I was destined for greatness and that I had a purpose in the world and was born to make a difference.

This was another turning point in my life, but this time things were beginning to look up and my trajectory was being altered. This woman who was strategically and divinely placed in my life was helping me transform into the person that she knew I had the potential to be. It was during this time that I saw the "roots" being positioned to provide me with the foundational supports I needed to become grounded so that I would not drift away from future goals and aspirations. Dr. Dorse Cleveland was a clear example of a caring adult who invested time, energy, and hope in me because she believed in me and had high expectations for me. Teachers who hold high expectations for their students create positive atmospheres for their students (Ladson-Billings, 2009). Consequently, students internalize these feelings and feel they are capable and act accordingly. Teachers need to recognize that their views of students can negatively or positively impact their students' academic success and to constantly engage in self-reflection to ensure they are always holding high expectations for their students (Hollis & Goings, 2017).

Dr. Dorse Cleveland worked with me throughout high school, placing me in activities, checking in and checking up on me, helping me process through tough situations, encouraging me to attend church, signing me up for plays, attending my awards ceremonies or events; and she even would take me places with her family. I now understand the importance of exposure and being able to experience different things other than my usual surroundings. As a student from a marginalized population, having my mentor expose me to numerous experience helped to increase my expectations to want to pursue a career and higher education at the postsecondary level (Hollis, 2016). It was as if I was finally getting the positive attention from a caring adult that I had longed for and cried out for. She and I developed a strong bond over the years. I slowly began to change and I was no longer getting into fights or getting suspended; I was even getting comments such as a "pleasure to teach" on my reports.

Even though some aspects of my life at home had improved, it was hard putting on a façade and pretending that everything was all right at home, the one place that was supposed to be full of love, safety, security, and support. So, I was still facing the trouble at home, while encountering negativity at school as well. Let us not forget that I was also trying to maintain academically so that I could go away to college. Thus, having Dr. Dorse Cleveland in my life as a supportive factor was integral in helping me develop the roots that I needed so that I would not drift away from my destiny when the time came for me to use my wings to fly. She continued to place me into programs, help me with scholarship and college applications, and just ensure that I was staying on top of my studies. I ended up getting a full ride to Davidson College in Davidson, NC. I did not want to attend that college at first because I did not want to leave my siblings behind.

During my time in college, I continued to follow the sage advice of my mentor and she and I had the best of relationships. It was during interactions with students, faculty, and community members, as well as in times of isolation and intrapersonal reflection, when I was able to initially articulate and make meaning of my identity. I had to define and examine for myself how I wanted to describe my identity as an African American woman. It was challenging as I found myself often having more questions than answers. It was as if hearing my mentor's voice reminding me of her wisdom helped me recognize the importance of having roots that would help me excel and succeed, despite the doubt and obstacles I encountered. I kept hearing my mentor's voice: "Trust in the Lord and lean not unto your own understanding," she would remind me. I tried so many times to show strength so others would not think I was weak. I found myself in daily battles with racism and prejudice. I was angry, indecisive, and, most of all, tired. I was angry because I found myself in isolation. In my new life as a college student, I often found myself struggling with the feeling that I was the only one here having to prove my worth and value as a woman of color in academia. Consequently, I had to find a refuge among other people who understood my journey. This became important as I experienced many emotions and even became depressed to the point of wanting to give up. I began to question who I was and if I was truly where I needed to be.

I was torn between being "too Black," "too hood," or "too ghetto" for the students of color, but not being White enough for the Whites. It was a draining process—living in two worlds and not fitting in either. I was tired of explaining myself to my family, peers, professors, and so on; tired of being perceived as the angry Black woman; tired of being the only one to speak up in class and show up and mobilize others when there was racism on campus. But most of all, I was tired of other people not understanding my experience, including members of my immediate family. My mentor, who consistently provided me with the support that I needed to overcome my bouts with depression and doubt, always reminded me to remember who I am and whose I am. I was tired of trying to figure out how to show up and who to show up as on which day. Just as I would encounter success or happiness in my journey through college life, I would quickly be reminded by instances of racism on campus that I was still in fact an African American woman, regardless of the positions or titles that I held. I came into college believing the environment was supposed to be a place where my mind would be challenged, where I would be nourished, my identity and purpose nurtured, and where my interactions with others would lead to growth and development. I was longing for the "home" away from home and the nurturing environment that I so desperately needed to experience.

Many people often seemed surprised to hear that I was pursuing a master's degree in spite of all of the things that I had gone through in my lifetime. It was rare to hear about young African American females who grow up in adverse circumstances and without a father figure to accomplish the goals that I had accomplished so far. My educational journey became more complex as I matriculated through several educational settings, including my graduate school experience. My educational journey became more complex as I matriculated through several educational settings, including my graduate school experience and attaining my doctorate. During this time, conversations with my mentor who understood the journey kept me focused and made it easy to stay motivated. Although the darkness of discrimination and racism always followed, the stories and conversations provided a safe haven from the negativity and a connection to my support system, which gave me the strength that I needed to face my obstacles. I currently have my PhD and am a tenure-track professor as a result of the wings and roots that were placed in my path. As I revisit my educational journey, it becomes clear that I have not made it to the mountaintop yet, even though I have had to move several mountains along the way.

As I embark upon this new obstacle in my life—being an early career scholar and woman of color in the academy—I am reminded that life teaches us many lessons; however, it is what we learn from those lessons that matter. Would I be where I am without my wings or my roots? Probably not, but I am so glad that there were people who took a vested interest in me and that I encountered some of the experiences (positive and negative) that I did because they truly helped shape and mold me into the first-generation female professor of color I currently am. I will never forget where I came from. A large part of my motivation for attaining a doctorate and becoming a professor was so that I could have something and some way to give back. I really see my role as being twofold: I am striving to improve my situation, while at the same time working to improve the situation of the next generation. I am grateful that my mentor and many other adults have supported me and given me roots and wings so that I could be successful on my educational journey. These roots and wings have been integral in the growth that I have made over the years and the decisions that I made to pursue an advanced degree and to become a professor at the college level.

I hope that my auto-ethnographic account conveys the strength, resourcefulness, and resilience of an African American first-generation female student, who despite obstacles and barriers, continues to overcome. I want educators to understand the social and cultural context of mentoring and what it truly means to have someone who looks like you but is no relation and has a vested interest in you enough to mentor you. I hope that through my journey others will be inspired to overcome obstacles and become successful. I hope my words will remind mentors and educators that they are critical to a child's trajectory. My relationship with my mentor showed that having a caring adult in your life can help to turn the trajectory around for a child whom society considers "at-risk." However, with the supports of a mentor and a caring adult in place, that same child can go from at-risk to at-opportunity in a matter of years. Although educators are unable to control many of the risk factors students face, they can gain an understanding of the protective factors that help students to succeed. Teachers can foster resilience in their students by developing a caring and personal relationship with their students by having positive and high expectations, while providing the necessary supports for students to reach those expectations; and by providing meaningful opportunities to students. In this way, educators (like my mentor) can provide the roots to ground students while empowering them with the wings to soar above their obstacles.

REFERENCES

Bernard, B. (2004). *Resiliency: What we have learned.* San Francisco, CA: West Ed.

Gay, G. (2000). *Culturally responsive teaching: Theory, research, and practice.* New York, NY: Teachers College Press.

Hollis, T. (2016). Wings and roots: Perspectives on resilience and academic success in education. In G. Wiggan (Ed.), *Dreaming of a place called home: Local and international perspectives on teacher education and school diversity* (pp. 101–119). Rotterdam, The Netherlands: Sense.

Hollis, T. (2019). Building bridges and fostering hope: Helping traumatized children learn through trauma-sensitive practices at the middle school level. *North Carolina Middle Level Education Journal, 32*(1). Retrieved from: https://ncmlejournal.org/fall-2019-v321#724d21a9-ddde-4c85-ac88 8bbed15621a8

Hollis, T., & Goings, R. B. (2017). Keeping the dream through the CARE model: Examining strategies to bridge the gaps in education among urban youth. In W. T. Pink & G. W. Noblit (Eds.), *Second international handbook of urban education* (pp. 887–905). New York, NY: Springer International.

Masten, A. S. (1999). Resilience comes of age: Reflections on the past and outlook for the next generation of research. In M. D. Glantz, J. Johnson, & L. Huffman (Eds.), *Resilience and development: Positive life adaptations* (pp. 289–296). New York, NY: Plenum.

CHAPTER 7

TRYING A DIFFERENT APPROACH

The Influential Power of Mrs. Taylor and Mr. Johnson in Seeing an Ugly Duck Turn Into a Swan

James T. Jackson

A child born into an unhealthy home environment and a socio-political system of racial segregation, known as Jim Crow, in Hodges, South Carolina in 1952, had little chance of becoming anything but a common laborer, even though he dreamed of something better and would often spend nights standing in the backyard of the sharecropper framed house, that his mother and nine siblings occupied. He would often look upon the lights that shined from afar and wondered where they came from. While he dreamed and wondered, the reality of his life always returned to the environment of struggle, poverty, violence, and mistreatment because of his "Blackness" and his being a "bastard child." This was my life. The reality of my early experience often left me feeling like an ugly duckling. It is difficult to navigate spaces and places when you are viewed from the lens of being poor, a

The Impact of Classroom Practices, pages 65–76

"bastard child," and dark skinned. Back in 1952, when I was born, people with dark skin were often relegated to a position simply because of their color. Jim Crow laws made it difficult for all Black people, but being dark skinned was another form of segregation within the Black community.

This chapter recounts the influential ways in which two of my teachers, Ms. Taylor, my sixth-grade teacher, and Mr. Johnson, one of my high school choral teachers saw beyond the ugliness of the duck to help give life to a swan. It ends with some recommendations for educators to consider as they work to influence the lives of children.

A CONTEXT FOR THE UGLINESS OF THE DUCK

Having been born into the segregated south and a dysfunctional home, not much was expected of me or members of my family. By the time I started school in 1958, none of my older siblings had graduated high school, nor was my mother a high school graduate. However, there was some hope for me and two of my younger siblings; but it would not be sustained. By the time we got to high school, the younger brother, by 2 years, had dropped out; and an older sister, who got pregnant during the summer after her junior year, left school, after the first semester of her senior year. This was rather devastating to me because she had shown such promise academically and socially, and I had used her as an example of what I could become. Nonetheless, I persisted; even though I did not know anything about what I wanted to do. The standard for my family was that children would attend school long enough to read at a basic level and then go to work. Education was not seen as a valuable commodity. However, I knew I did not want to be like my sisters and brothers. I wanted to at least finish high school, for it was here that I flourished and became a little more focused on doing well, despite the odds, but that was not the beginning. Research on the impact of a negative environment on a child's self-esteem and behavior regularly indicates that a myriad of problems can result. The consequences of growing up in a household with few resources and the socio-political construct of the Jim Crow south did not give me much hope. The fact that I was poor, dark skinned, and without a father figure had me thinking negatively of myself early. The internal struggle of not being worthy of love, coupled with being treated differently because of segregation and skin color, created a mental schema that left me feeling like I was an ugly duckling.

Having been born to a widowed mother, who lost her first husband in a tragic auto accident because of his addiction to alcohol, made me wonder why I was conceived. Nonetheless, I grew up without much direction and poor examples for the future. You see, in addition to my mother being a widow, she was also a sharecropper (someone who farmed the land by planting, growing, chopping, and picking cotton in exchange for a place to stay and money to buy food and other essentials to live). I realize now that this arrangement was one step away from slavery, but at the time, and as a young boy, I was not aware of its impact; even though, I did notice the difference in treatment of Black people as a result of the Jim Crow laws. For example, while I never experienced a lynching, which was prevalent in the south during the 1950s, I do remember the numerous visits from what we called "night riders." I later learned that they were the Ku Klux Klan. These individuals' primary goal was to frighten Black people into submission in order to maintain the status quo of White superiority. There were many times that crosses were burned, and Black men and teenage boys were beaten. While I never witnessed any of my brothers suffering this atrocity, they did spend significant time in the local jail for fighting and drunkenness, and sometimes were assigned to the Chain Gang for their misdeeds. My mother's response to all of this, particularly the visits by the Ku Klux Klan, was to direct her children to put the oil lamps out, our source of light, for there was no electricity or indoor plumbing, to sit quietly in the dark until the terrorizers left. Her response to the seemingly weekly jailing of one of her older boys, was to have the man who owned the land that she sharecropped bail them out on any given Sunday morning, which further provided a sense of enslavement because this additional burden of being indebted obligated us to plant, grow, chop, and pick more cotton. The fact that my mother sought support to have the landowner rescue one of her three older sons from jail almost weekly was really a "sore eye" for the family and continued until the second oldest son got into a fight with my mother's youngest brother, Uncle Alonzo. According to accounts, Elbert, the second oldest son of my mother was drunk, got into an argument with my uncle at a local "juke joint," cut a major artery, and my uncle bled to death. This tragedy created a feeling of loss for me because my uncle was my supporter, and even though he was often drunk from alcohol consumption, he was always nice to me and tried to serve as a positive role model. He talked, let me talk, and he listened. I often wonder if he had lived, what impact would he have had on my life and I on his.

My life as a young child growing up in the south during the 1950s was fraught with many hardships. One of these hardships was living in a wooden framed house without insulation. I previously mentioned that there was no electricity and indoor plumbing. There was also no central heating or air (I suppose that is why I don't need much heat in the winter or air conditioning in the summer today). During the winter months, my mother would instruct the younger children to use whatever materials we could find to plug opened holes in the house to keep the cold air out. As there was no central heating source, one room was often used by the family to stay warm, which was done by a fireplace, later a cast iron heater, that was filled with wood or coal. The other rooms had no heat, so before bed, bricks would be heated, wrapped in a towel or other pieces of cloth and placed in the bed to provide heat. We would dress in pajamas, stand in front of the fireplace or heater to get warm, and then run and get in bed. Because there were so many of us living under one roof, sleeping two or three to a bed helped to promote warmth. In the summer, every door and window were opened to allow cool breezes to blow through the house. Moreover, food was often scarce. To help with the food supply, my brothers would often go hunting and fishing. This produced some interesting meals and food choices. For example, there was a time that my mother served a roasted opossum that was surrounded by sweet potato slices and sat in the middle of the dining table, which was in the kitchen, across from the wood burning stove. The meal may have been okay, but when I discovered that the "big rat," had been cooked with its head attached, I couldn't and wouldn't eat! It were these incidents that taught me early how to subsist on minimal food and be selective about what I consume today.

Another hardship of being born poor and Black in the segregated south was the lack of opportunity. Since my family was poor and had little formal education, it meant that its financial well-being was dependent upon how much cotton could be grown and picked. Regardless of how productive the family was, there was never enough money to free us from the clutches of what seemed like slavery. Nonetheless, after some years, my mother decided to leave the cotton field to become a domestic worker, whose exploits have been documented so well in both the movie and book titled, *The Help*. I was about 12 years old when my mother made the decision to leave. However, before this occurred, I had my first experience in public school. It was 3 years after the *Brown v. Board of Education*, Topeka, Kansas decision. While I was unaware of how this court case would impact the education of Black children, I was only six, I knew something was not right. On the first day of school, rather than jump on the bus in front of the wooden framed house, me, my younger brother, and my youngest sister, had to walk six miles or more in order to catch the bus. This would happen regardless of weather conditions. There were many days that we did not attend school. Perhaps this was one of the reasons I only attended school about 80 days of the 180 required by the district. I am also certain that this is the reason I had to repeat first grade.

When I arrived at North Hodges Elementary School in 1958, I was taken aback by a comment that was made by one of the teachers, as the students gathered to enter the building. The teacher said, "There is one of those Jackson boys." I did not understand the context then, but I knew that I did not like what I heard. I would later learn that my older brothers had presented tremendous behavior problem for some of the teachers and this teacher thought I would be just as bad. As a result of this knowledge, I decided that I would not be a problem. Rather, I remained quiet in Mrs. Thomas' first grade classroom. I was so afraid to speak up and participate that I never asked to use the bathroom and would often wet my pants. During recess, I would stand on the sidelines and watch other children play. I had no concept of what it meant to be a happy and free-spirited child. The preoccupation with my life at home, the lack of resources, having to wear the same clothes 5 days a week, having no textbooks (parents had to pay for rental of textbooks back then) and some other misfortunes really left me feeling anxious and uncertain. I now know that I was a child who operated from the internal dimension of behavior and could have benefitted from special support, but back in 1958, no one thought that a young Black boy needed special attention. Being a young Black boy, who thought he was not wanted by his father, created an internal struggle so severe that belief in myself was non-existent. I only lived because I did not know what else to do. I would often have bad dreams at night, wet the bed, and developed fears and phobias about many things. I was particularly afraid to cross bridges as I thought they would collapse. I still have some queasiness about crossing major bridges today. However, not being able to discuss my feelings with a significant adult, as most children born in Black rural southern communities, in the 1950s, and earlier were not encouraged to talk about how they felt. They were to be seen and not heard. Therefore, I started to use my creative energy as an outlet to soothe a broken soul. The result was an exploration of creating objects out of the red clay (we called it mud) that permeated the landscape of my community.

While my first year in school was difficult, I also questioned why I had to pass a school, designated for White children, close to my house, to attend one for Black children that was farther away. This socio-political dynamic further impacted my fragile self-esteem, made me feel unimportant, unequal, and uncared for. Having negative images of myself because of environmental and socio-political mores that did not promote a sense of acceptance and justice, left me wondering about my trajectory. Nonetheless, I propelled myself to the second grade, after having spent 2 years in first grade. I managed to sustain myself, although much had not changed. I did have access to textbooks and the school bus was now stopping at the wooden framed house and taking us to school. We no longer had to walk six miles in any weather conditions. I performed well enough academically and had become a little more socially involved, that I was able to advance to the third grade, where I met Ms. Pearl Miller. She provided a comfortable and structured classroom and promoted a sense of discipline. I was in a "good space." However, when I got to fourth grade, the pressure of having lost my Uncle Alonzo and knowing that one of my brothers had killed him made me spiral out of control. I no longer internalized my feelings and thoughts, but operated from the externalized dimension of behavior to the point that

I assaulted other classmates and the teacher. I became angry both because of my uncle's death and how my meager existence did not match the lives of my classmates; some of them with fathers, who had good jobs, cars, and could afford things for their children. I resented this, so I stole, but would often return the items when my conscience got the best of me.

As I entered fifth grade, I carried the angry thoughts and negative behaviors with me, but I had stopped stealing. However, because I was being bullied and eventually sexually assaulted by an older boy, the negative behaviors increased. Feeling horrified and not knowing what to do or who to talk with, I kept that secret until I was 28 years of age, when I shared it with some Navy buddies aboard a ship in Norfolk, Virginia. I chose not to tell family members, because I was afraid that my mother would hold me responsible and punish me. I also thought that I would be further ostracized by brothers and sisters, because I was regularly called disparaging names because of my bastard status and the complexion of my skin. I became so tired of being misunderstood and mistreated, that I would often run away from home and spend hours in the woods to find some relief. I believed that my mother really hated me because of the absence of my father. However, before I reached a total meltdown and acted on thoughts of suicide, I was advanced to the sixth grade, where I met Mrs. Taylor. This tall, light-complexion lady with glasses, had a classroom structure that promoted a sense of community, classroom engagement, student responsibility, and so many other qualities that were helpful for a troubled child. She also saw the value that theater and dramatic performance could play in developing the lives of children. Mr. Johnson, my high school choral teacher for 4 years, did a similar thing with singing. He too saw what singing and being part of a focused group could do to a young man who had endured so much. Both these individuals help give life to the ugly duck so that he could blossom into a swan.

THE INFLUENCES OF MRS. TAYLOR AND MR. JOHNSON IN HELPING THE UGLY DUCK BECOME A SWAN

Hans Christian Andersen's 1843 classic, *"The Ugly Duckling,"* recounts the puzzlement of a mother duck who wonders why one of her ducklings looked so differently and larger than her other off springs, as she professed her love for all her ducklings, despite their differences. The ugly duckling, who was a swan, was berated, which resulted in him feeling ashamed. The mother duck, embarrassed because of the differences in her children, demanded that the ugly duckling confine himself to a specific area of the pond so that he would not be seen by others. The treatment by the mother duck and the taunts of the other birds forced the ugly duckling to wander away as he thought no one wanted him. However, one day the ugly duckling happened upon a group of birds, other swans, that look liked him. It was with this group that he found his place and acceptance. Mrs. Taylor's classroom was like the ugly duckling finding other swans. She created a classroom environment that spoke to acceptance, cooperation, community, responsibility, discipline, and structure. She was a strong disciplinarian, whose objectives were clear. She communicated a sense of fairness, but also demanded personal accountability. She capitalized on the uniqueness of her students and celebrated that in the way she spoke, shared her knowledge and expectations. She also provided outlets to help students realize their uniqueness. She was the first person to allow me to see how valuable theater and the art of performance could be used to alter one's trajectory, regardless of the negative baggage that was acquired along the way. She did this by casting me in my first ever play, because she discovered that I could sing. While I never got to perform in front of the audience of community members, because I didn't have transportation to get me to the night performance. I was devastated and disappointed, yet I understood that because my family had limited resources, I didn't question the lack of support, but I cried and questioned why my life was so cruel and why no responsible adult felt the need to support me. I thought that I had failed Mrs. Taylor and disappointed my class and school. Nonetheless, when I returned to school the next day, Mrs. Taylor never asked why I did not attend the performance. Rather, she embraced me and conducted her classroom instruction as she normally did. Perhaps she knew more about my home environment and the struggles that I was experiencing than I realized. She continued to encourage and place me in activities that allowed me to use my ability to sing and develop more positive skills and behavior. Because of the commitment of Mrs. Taylor, I used these opportunities to reshape and reframe my life. I created a new character for myself. The creation of this new character helped to present a less angry young man and motivated him to find ways to relate with other students and form positive rather than destructive connections. The recognition that I received from being featured in school talent shows propelled me to change my negative ways. This recognition would later move into the community, where I often sang at churches. I became active in the local 4-H Club, which gave me an opportunity to develop my leadership skills and become a regional song leader. This newfound life even led to other teachers, at North Hodges Elementary School, to become involve in assisting me. Mrs. Miller, my third-grade teacher, who had become principal of the school, when I was in sixth grade, started to provide me with more assistance and encouraged me to participate in 4-H competitions and would provide me with transportation and resources to help become a ribbon winner. I was a new person and I took those things with me as I transitioned to Brewer High School, the high school for Black students in Greenwood, South Carolina, in the Fall of 1964.

When I arrived at Brewer, I was still a bit timid about my existence. Here I was, a boy from the country and not having a strong sense of confidence, expected to interact with young people from many socio-economic backgrounds. I was a little embarrassed and afraid. It did not help that the name James Jackson was also a part of my persona. As the new junior high students gathered in the auditorium, to be assigned to a homeroom class, students in upper grades were there to assist us in getting us to the classrooms to which we were assigned. When my name was called, I heard much snickering. I became self-conscious and wondered why that was. I would later learn that the snickering occurred because my name was the same as an older student who lived his life openly gay. While I did not understand and resented the snickering, I tried to remain positive, but the taunting of teenagers sometimes hurt and led to negative encounters. After having been ridiculed because of my name too many times, I reverted to fighting and trying to get revenge. The consequences of this led to a few days of suspension from school. I was again devastated but learned from the experience. When I returned to school, I vowed that I would not fight again and made efforts to do a different thing. With the encouragement of my eighth grade English teacher, I entered an oratorical and declamation contest. I used my anger about being ridiculed for my name to connect to a deep emotional pain to breathe life into the performance on the night of the contest. I was declared one of the winners! My female cousin, from my father's side of the family, was the other winner. After that win, I gathered the courage to do other things in the area of performance; the result was my participating in a talent show that had been spearheaded by one of the physical education teachers at the school. When she asked me if I wanted to participate, she told me that one of her friends, who represented a recording company would be in the audience and that he possibly would be looking for new talent. I agreed to do it, but had some trepidation, because this was a much larger adventure than previous ones. I performed my song, and while I did not win the talent show, the recording representative did ask me if I was interested in recording. My response to him, mostly out of ignorance and knowing that my family would not be supportive, was "No." I regret that decision now, but when a young man comes from an environment like mine and there is no one to provide guidance, mistakes are often made. Nonetheless, one day as I stood alone in the schoolyard of Brewer, I overheard the choir, under the direction of Mr. Johnson, practicing. I listened to this sound several days, until I finally mustered up the courage and went to his office, in the basement of the school auditorium and told him I wanted to audition for the choir. Afterall, singing had become my drug of choice. There were many evenings that I would stroll the streets of Hodges, by this time my mother had moved to the city part of the town, entertaining myself as there was little else to do. Mr. Johnson auditioned me and accepted my voice as one of the singers in the bass section of the choir. It was a marvelous undertaking and brought another dimension to help me become something more than I thought I could.

Being a member of Mr. Johnson's choir provided many things. First, it gave me an opportunity to be among students who had a similar focus in that we all loved to sing. Prior to joining the choir, I wasn't very active at Brewer. Living outside the city of Greenwood, which is where the high school was, and not having transportation to travel the more than eight miles, I was reluctant to become involved. Being a part of the choir allowed me socialization and an opportunity to be involved during school hours.

Another benefit of being in the choir was the chance to view Mr. Johnson as a father figure. As someone who operated with a precision for excellence, discipline, commitment, preparation, and a sense of caring and love for his students, I saw in him someone whose behaviors I could mimic. I had never had the experience of connecting with a Black man who was a professional and demonstrated the kind of characteristics that I would realize in my own life. I think if I had not been a part of Mr. Johnson's choir, I would not have ever developed the kind of commitment to the work that I currently do as a university professor.

Mr. Johnson provided me exposure outside of the small town that I was accustomed to seeing. It was through his connection to Benedict College (he graduated from there) that I was able to take my first major trip outside of Hodges and subsequently experience what it was like to be on a college campus, something that I thought I would never do. While at Benedict, we not only performed a wonderful concert, but for some of us, it was our first time seeing Columbia, the capital city of South Carolina, which is where Benedict is located. This trip, although short, gave me my second thoughts about what life might be like away from Hodges.

The discipline that Mr. Johnson exhibited in working with the choir was exceptional! He demanded of his singers to always be prepared, know their parts, sing them well, and have a presence that indicated confidence. During rehearsals, he would often walk among the risers and listen to individuals sing to make sure that parts were correct. If singers did not produce the sound that he expected, he would ask them to leave the risers and sit in the audience and listen to other singers so that they could get it right. This activity was especially harsh when the choir was preparing for a concert. The passion that he displayed was sometimes frightening, but he always managed to comfort those singers who might have felt embarrassed for being pulled from the risers. Nonetheless, we all knew he loved us and wanted us to do our best. I believe he knew the importance of Black Excellence and he wanted that for us. It just didn't seem like that at the time.

THE SWAN'S LESSONS FROM MRS. TAYLOR AND MR. JOHNSON TO EDUCATORS

Children who are born into circumstances that they cannot control, often make choices about how to live their lives. They may choose to focus on the negative influences of these experiences and spiral out of control, like most of my siblings; or they may decide to endure the challenges and think about how to use them as motivators to become something better. Someone who steps in to provide guidance can ensure the latter more than the former.

Mrs. Taylor and Mr. Johnson served that role for me and I believe that there are lessons for other educators to learn. Therefore, the following thoughts are recommended for both new and seasoned educators, in hopes that they will make it possible for many swans to flourish, regardless of their beginning. The power of a significant and authentic teacher can be the difference between success and failure for a troubled and misdirected student. The lessons are:

1. Accept students, regardless of their differences. Students come to the learning environment from a variety of backgrounds, have different needs, issues, and so on. Many teachers often see themselves as authority figures, who will hold students accountable, apply affirmations when there is accountability, and eventually move into the realm of acceptance. Bianco (2002) has suggested that this order should be reversed:
   - Acceptance: I accept you unconditionally. Your background, parents, lifestyle, skills, and habits are all real, but do not infringe on my total commitment to you.
   - Accountable: As your teacher, I am accountable for this year's academic, social, and emotional growth.
   - Affirmation: I see you as a work in progress and I will make a considerable contribution to your future success.
   - Authority: I will use my authority to be your advocate and be viewed as a valuable person in your life (p. 13).

   Children need to know that they are more important than their problems/behaviors. Unconditional acceptance coupled with structure and humane consequences, provide students with an opportunity to experience restorative justice and find healthy ways to contribute to the classroom community. Richards (2018) believes individuals who have "a chance to rebuild relationships after a misstep and to foster empathy, attunement, and accountability helps the whole community to feel safe and more connected" (p. 3).
2. Focus on students' strengths. Every student has something to offer, but if educators concentrate more on the deficits and not the

strengths, they may miss an opportunity to see gifts and talents that may be useful to help build a sense of classroom community. Boykin and Noguera (2011) have referred to these talents and gifts as assets that children bring to the classroom environment. Moreover, the New York University Steinhardt School of Culture, Education and Human Development (2018) has suggested that asset-based teaching seeks to unbridle students' potential and focus on their talents by highlighting strengths more than the deficits. The teacher who focuses on the strengths of children more than the deficits, can potentially create self-empowered individuals, who can do good and find ways, with guidance, to engage in more appropriate behaviors.

3. Find alternative and unusual teaching methods to engage and access students' knowledge. Students are more than their cognitive abilities and because many of them possess social-emotional problems that hinder this ability, other approaches might need to be employed by teachers to meet children where they are. If a child has a passion for the arts, perhaps that might be the method that the teacher utilizes to motivate growth in other areas. Both Mrs. Taylor and Mr. Johnson used art forms to change my trajectory. Perhaps they realized the truism that Renzulli (1973) spoke of so many years ago when he suggested that creative ability is one component to his three-ring concept of giftedness and that children from culturally different backgrounds often display a higher level of creative ability. Moreover, the National Endowment for the Arts (2015) has reported that the use of arts in educating children has multiple benefits, to include pro-social skills, cooperation, independence, emotional regulation, and reduction in both externalizing and internalizing behaviors.
4. Expose students to the unfamiliar. Many students from under resourced homes and communities don't have the luxury of experiencing the world beyond these places. Good teachers, like Mrs. Taylor and Mr. Johnson, expose children to worlds unknown so that they might gain a new perspective. When I taught public school, it amazed me that students who lived near major metropolitan areas had never experienced them. Mrs. Taylor and Mr. Johnson both saw the need to introduce students to worlds beyond their home communities. Prior to meeting these two amazing teachers, I had never traveled to a major city. However, because of them I was able to visit my first college campus, fly on a plane to Washington, DC, and experience so many other things. Who would have ever thought that a young boy, born to a sharecropper mother, as a "bastard child," would one day sing at Carnegie Hall. I did not, but

> because of the early influences of Mrs. Taylor and Mr. Johnson, I did and have done so much more than I thought I could.

Good and effective teachers possess many qualities. The ones mentioned above are the most important that I learned from Mrs. Taylor and Mr. Johnson. Perhaps there are other lessons to be learned from my story, but teachers who practice unconditional acceptance, focus on students' strengths, use alternative ways to educate and engage students, and make a commitment to expose students to the unfamiliar, could be the catalyst to motivate them to look at and experience their lives differently. Maybe you can be the next teacher who will.

REFERENCES

Andersen, H. C. (1843). *The ugly duckling*. Copenhagen, Denmark: C.A. Reitzel.

Bianco, A. (2002). *One-minute discipline: Classroom management strategies that work*. San Francisco, CA: Jossey-Bass.

Boykin, A. W., & Noguera, P. (2011). *Creating the opportunity to learn: Moving from research to practice to close the achievement gap*. Alexandria, VA: Association for Supervision and Curriculum Development.

National Endowments for the Arts. (2015). *The arts in early childhood: Social emotional benefits of arts participation*. Washington, DC: Author.

New York University's Steinhardt School of Culture, Education, and Human Development. (2018). *An asset-based approach to education: What it is and why it matters*. New York, NY: Author. Retrieved from https://teachereducation.steinhardt.nyu.edu/an-asset-based-approach-to-education-what-it-is-and-why-it-matters/

Renzulli, J. S. (1973). Talent potential in minority group students. *Exceptional Children, 39*(6), 437–444.

Richards, J. (2018, September 4). How restorative justice helps students learn. *Edutopia*. Retrieved from https://www.edutopia.org/article/how-restorative-justice-helps-students-learn

CHAPTER 8

HIGH EXPECTATIONS

The Key Ingredient to Academic Success

Jubria Lewis

Teaching has always been considered a noble profession in the African American community. Teachers were revered by young people because of their position and status in the community, intellectual acumen, and ability to serve as role models. Teachers of African descent, when teaching students of African descent often find that the "hidden curriculum" requires them to focus on education as a means of "liberation" because they see themselves in the students that they are educating. These teachers often use culturally relevant pedagogies and curriculum to empower their students. These beliefs and approaches are the underpinnings to the high expectations that permeates the culture of the teacher's classroom and is the glue to the relationship that he or she establishes with each individual student. Culturally relevant pedagogies and curriculum address issues of access, inclusion, and racism in schools by empowering students socially, emotionally, and politically by using cultural referents to impart knowledge, skills, and attitudes" (Ladson Billings, 1992, p. 382). Similarly, they cultivate

The Impact of Classroom Practices, pages 77–83

a strong academic base, and foster students' positive self-worth and racial and cultural identities (Asante, 1991; Ladson Billings, 1992; Mudhabuti & Mudhabuti, 1991).

PURPOSE OF THE CHAPTER

The purpose of this chapter is to highlight Mr. Rener, a highly effective African-American male teacher and how he personified the principles of culturally relevant teaching through his high expectations for all students. The storytelling methodology of this chapter is structured in a manner that preservice teachers understand the need to develop deep relationships with their students, articulating high expectations to them and being deliberate on delivering on it in instruction, culture, and community. Finally, practitioners will be provided with key recommendations that support one in creating a positive climate for all students, particularly, Black and Brown students to thrive academically and socially.

A REFLECTION ON MY EARLY SCHOOLING YEARS

The start of each school year is often filled with such anticipation for many people. On one hand, parents are often overjoyed when their children return to school. On the other hand, teachers and school leaders are thrilled at another chance to empower an awaiting group of scholars with knowledge and skills, while fostering their love to become life-long learners. Moreover, students are mixed with emotions for endless reasons such as excitement to connect with friends in hope that they are in the same class or classes, nervous about attending a new school, or hopeful that they have the best teacher(s) based on the rumor mill from older friends and family members.

August of 1991 was no different for me as I looked forward to the sixth grade at St. Charles Elementary School in Jeanerette, a small, working class city in the Acadiana region of Louisiana. My excitement and anticipation existed because it was a 33% chance that I would have Mr. Rener as my teacher, one of the two African-American male teachers in my elementary school and one of three teachers in the sixth grade. The school orientation day was the launch of every academic year where all students and parents were invited to the school where you looked for your name on either apples, books, or some type of novelty on the teachers' doors to indicate where you will spend the next 180 days of your life. This school cultural event was the central focus of every students' phone conversation, park and playground chatter, or Sunday School whisper. Our conversations typically went like this, "I sure hope that I am in Mr. Rener's class. I hear that he is a fun teacher and you will do a lot of projects in his class." My friend chimed in with, "Me too, and our last names are close so we will sit by each other because they will put us in alphabetical order! But I hear that he does not play either. He expects a lot!"

The walk down the hallway seemed to take forever, as the sixth grade was the terminal grade at St. Charles Elementary School, and housed the oldest students in their own little enclave within the school. While walking down, the responses of students were evident of either their anticipation or disappointment in who their instruction will be led by for the academic school year. My heart began to palpitate at the speed of light as I got closer to the sixth-grade corridor. Walking with my mom, she delayed the reveal as she spoke to all of my previous teachers because she built great relationships with them as a parent and as a fellow colleague at the local high school in our community. I realized as I walked with my mom and greeted all of my former teachers that all of them from second through fifth grade looked like me. This not only worked in my favor because we shared the same hue and cultural experiences, but it had an impact on my overall educational attainment. Gershenson, Hart, Hyman, Lindsay, and Papageorge (2018) found that Black students who had one Black teacher by third grade were 13% more likely to enroll in college, while those who had two Black teachers were 32% more likely. The moment of truth as I reached the doors of the three sixth grade teachers. I went straight to Mr. Rener's door to look for my name and before I could even begin searching, I could hear his deep voice say to me, "Yep, Jubria, you are in the right place." My reaction was a clear indication that I got my wish as I screamed, "Yes, and my gestures motioned like I just scored a touchdown in the Super Bowl's fourth quarter. Though I have had African American teachers from second through fifth grade, this was really special because I nailed an African American male teacher; a rare breed in both rural Louisiana and the nation.

The most underrepresented demographic of teachers in America are African American males at a startling 1%, equating to approximately 35,000 teachers in our public schools, with most being at the middle and high school levels (Aud et al., 2013; Lewis, 2006; Lewis & Toldson, 2013). Having no knowledge of this scarcity as an 11-year-old boy, I was thrilled to start the new school year. The school year was off to a great start and I recall every morning being excited about another day of learning. Mr. Rener just did an amazing job of creating a culture of care, respect, appreciation, joy, and risk-taking. During that time, I could not necessarily articulate my feelings of these elements that are quite evident in our classroom environment, but I knew that our experiences were different than in some of the other classes. Friends would share stories of their classroom cultures on the playground, but it seems as if we were able to walk with an increased level of pride due to the energy and vibe that Mr. Rener cultivated in the classroom amongst teacher to student and student to student. Our teacher's expectations were delivered through modeling his culture of care both verbal and nonverbal. Though classrooms are depicted as neutral sites where social and academic learning occurs, the social context of a classroom affects the learning that happens in that classroom (Young & Smith, 1997). One social factor is the relationship between teacher and student; however, if this relationship is caring, then students academically and socially benefit (Birch & Ladd, 1997). Though I knew I had a special relationship with Mr. Rener, it became evident quickly that he had developed a special relationship with each student and then collectively as a class community. He truly made a concerted effort to exemplify what the National Council for the Accreditation of Teacher Education, also referred to as NCATE (National Council for Accreditation of Teacher Education, 2008), requires in its teacher disposition of caring for their students not only materially, but also socially, emotionally, relationally, and academically.

Mr. Rener's spirit of caring was anchored in his commitment to high expectations of us, and we felt the symbiotic relationship with the two. His caring allowed us to deepen the bonds of trust in our classroom. This was pivotal in being able to understand and feel the high expectations that our teacher had for us. His high expectations became the heartbeat of our classroom, particularly in his approaches to teaching and learning and our disposition to learning. I can vividly remember receiving a B in reading and I was crushed because I just unequivocally knew that I deserved an A. Before going out for recess one day, Mr. Rener called me back because he sensed that I was not as participatory in class and did not show up well in class. He inquired about what was bothering me and I blurted out with a mixture of frustration, anger, hurt, and disappointment, "You gave me a B in reading and I am the best reader in this class!" His response was also a combination of a teacher and a father with, "You are indeed an outstanding student Jubria, but I have told you a number of times that you are rushing through your work to finish first to have others believe that you are smart and that is not smart to do. You earned that B; however, I am expecting you to work to your greatest potential and earn that A you desire." His words at that time did not resolve the A that I wanted in the moment, however, I worked hard from that point on because his words were worth and value given the relationship we had established and his unwavering expectations around student achievement.

Mr. Rener's degree of cultural competence assisted in his effectiveness in advancing student achievement in his classroom. Ladson-Billings (1995) refers to cultural competence as the ability to function effectively in one's own culture of origin. For African American students, which we were the majority in Mr. Rener's classroom, it meant understanding those aspects of our culture and possess the ability to communicate and relate to other members of the cultural group (Gay & Baber, 1987). Our classroom conversations were never short of discussing college life on Historically Black Colleges & Universities (HBCU), as one was an alma mater of Mr. Rener. He used this connection to encourage us to set our aim on college education, while relating it to those schools that resonated at beacons of excellence in our communities, such as Grambling State University, Southern University, Xavier University of Louisiana, and Dillard University. He would further share his stories of being in a Black Greek-lettered fraternity, Omega Psi Phi and how they supported each other academically and built a bond of brotherhood. These anecdotal lessons were not part of the taught curriculum, but it allowed African American children to see themselves in college, particularly those that have educated our ancestors, parents, and other members of our village. His expectations were that I want you to see yourself in me and pushed us to work hard to maintain high scholastic achievement, because we were college bound.

PRACTICAL RECOMMENDATIONS FOR TEACHERS

As Mr. Rener was my first African American male teacher in my K–12 career, it has left an indelible mark on my life and what I established as a benchmark for my career. It is without a doubt the reason that I became an educator and started my career as a fifth-grade teacher; I too, became the first African American male teacher for many students. Furthermore, I was able to share my experiences in college both at a PWI and an HBCU, pledging Alpha Phi Alpha Fraternity with my 100% African American students. My high expectations for my students were similar to those that Mr. Rener had for us and also those that I developed in my own personal professional journey. As a preservice teacher, it is necessary to understand that having high expectations is the key ingredient to academic achievement. The following strategies should be the underpinning to your pedagogical approaches as well as your classroom culture:

1. Develop a strong belief in the learning capacity of all students and adopt a growth mindset around teaching and learning. Grounding your north star in that All means All.
2. Recognize that each parent has sent you their best and it is incumbent upon the educational community to articulate the high

expectations that you have for students in your approaches, words, actions, systems, and policies.

3. Deliver an instructional program that is rigorous, while providing the supports and scaffolds for students who will struggle at various points during the learning process.
4. Establish a college-going culture for the entire community of students where they can envision their success in post-secondary educational pursuits
5. Provide quality on-going, explicit feedback to students throughout the academic year on their glows, grows, and goals.

Though this may not be an exhaustive list of strategies that should be adopted as a preservice teacher, it will be a launchpad for success and will strengthen your practice and provision of services.

REFERENCES

Asante, M. (1991). The Afrocentric idea in education. *Journal of Negro Education, 60*(2), 170–180.

Aud, S., Hussar, W., Johnson, F., Kena, G., Roth, E., Manning, E., Wang, X., . . . Zhang, J. (2013). *The condition of education 2013* (NCES 2012-045). Washington, DC: U.S. Department of Education, National Center for Education Statistics.

Birch, S. H., & Ladd, G. W. (1997). The teacher–child relationship and children's early school adjustment. *Journal of School Psychology, 35*(1), 61–79. https://doi.org/10.1016/s0022-4405(96)00029-5

Gay, G., & Baber, W. (1987). *Expressively Black: The cultural basis of ethnic identity.* New York, NY: Praeger.

Gershenson, S., Hart, C. M., Hyman, J., Lindsay, C., & Papageorge, N. (2018). *The long-run impacts of same-race teachers.* Retrieved from https://www.nber.org/system/files/working_papers/w25254/w25254.pdf

Ladson-Billings, G. (1992). Liberatory consequences of literacy: A case of culturally relevant instruction for African American students. *Journal of Negro Education, 61*(3), 378–391.

Ladson-Billings, G. (1995). Toward a theory of culturally relevant pedagogy. *American Educational Research Journal, 32*(3), 465–491.

Lewis, C. W. (2006). African American male teachers in public schools: An examination of three urban school districts. *Teachers College Record, 108*(2), 224–245.

Lewis, C. W., & Toldson, I. A. (Eds.). (2013). *Black male teachers: Diversifying the United States' teacher workforce.* Bingley, England: Emerald Group.

Mudhabuti, S., & Mudhabuti, H. (1991). *African-centered education: Its value, importance, and necessity in the development of Black children.* Chicago, IL: Third World Press.

National Council for Accreditation of Teacher Education. (2008). *Professional standards for accreditation of teacher preparation institutions.* Washington, DC: Author.

Young, B. A., & Smith, T. M. (1997). *The social context of education* (NCES 97-981). Washington, DC: U.S. Department of Education, Institute of Education Sciences, National Center for Education Statistics.

CHAPTER 9

IN HONOR OF SELMA WHITE

Marvin Lynn

I've written extensively about the work and lives of Black teachers. More specifically, I've spent my entire adult life either working as a Black male teacher or studying them. I've had the privilege of publishing my work on the work and lives of Black males in a number of prestigious academic journals. While I always acknowledge and publicly thank my own teachers who were so instrumental in my own development, I don't believe I've actually written about any of them in great detail. When the editors asked me to participate in this project, I was pleased that I would finally get the opportunity to blend the personal with the scholarly in a way that I had not done so before. While it's true that all scholarship is personal, it's also true that I have managed to maintain a degree of psychological and emotional distance from those whose work and lives I have studied. For example, I've never even desired to conduct research in my hometown of Chicago where I attended school from kindergarten through college. My research was set in New York, Los Angeles, Prince George's County, and Baltimore—both in Maryland. I had no personal ties to any of these places except that I either was obtaining a degree in an institution in one of those places or was employed as a professor there. Even when I took an academic job in Chicago, I did not endeavor to do research there. It was too close. I got too emotional

The Impact of Classroom Practices, pages 85–91

even at the thought of trying to understand, from a scholarly standpoint, the challenges facing Black educators in this deeply racist and heartless city of mine. I invested some energy into understanding more of the scholarship on Black education in Chicago when I taught a class on Black Education at UIC. I still didn't write about it.

Today, I am writing about a teacher who was like a family member—someone who invested so much of herself in me that I had no choice but to adore her back. The late Mrs. Selma White still holds a special place in my heart. Even as I write this, I worry about speaking so affectionately about a teacher. I don't want to give the wrong impression. But I also want to be honest about my genuine love for this selfless educator.

Mrs. White had a number of distinguishing features. Mrs. White was a southern Black woman with a bold face. She had long straight hair and did not usually wear makeup. She was also older than most teachers we encountered. No one knew Mrs. White's age. As high school students, we worked hard to try to figure it out. Sometimes fellow students in our class would ask and she'd reply, "Oh, I'm 150 years old." And then she'd quip, "Boy, don't you know you should never ask a lady her age?" And then she'd roar with laughter and walk away. When I met her in 1987, she was already at the end of a nearly 30-year teaching career. She was in her late 60s and was heading toward retirement. She had taught for many years at another high school on the southside of Chicago. She had not been teaching long at this new school. In fact, she was hired to replace a much-beloved music teacher who had become a school counselor. She was likely one of the oldest teachers on staff at Senn High School. This was a matter of interest for many students. It also gave her the license, as she put it, to say whatever she wanted to say. She felt no restrictions. She reminded me of the womanist teachers Annette Henry (1998) writes about in her study on Canadian women teachers. Alice Walker refers to a womanist as "a Black feminist... Usually referring to outrageous, audacious, courageous, or willful behavior... committed to the survival and the wholeness of an entire people" (Walker, 1983, as cited in Cannon, 1996). Walker describes the way the term emanates from the term "womanish"—a term used to describe a young Black girl who was acting "too grown" for her age. I suspect that Mrs. White, with her bold and sometimes outrageous personality, was likely accused of being "womanish" as a child. One cannot be certain. But I am certain about her commitment to me and all the students, who were mostly poor and working-class students of color, at Senn High School.

Like Annette Henry's teachers, Mrs. White worked "towards the cultural, political, educational, and spiritual survival of Black children" (Henry, 1998, p. 3). She not only helped us learn music, but she wanted to save our souls, to heal us, to liberate us, and render us completely free from the chains that bound so many of our ilk. Noted womanist theologian, Katie

Cannon (1996), talks about the suffering that Black women experience. It was clear to me that Mrs. White, as a Black womanist educator, suffered because of the state of education for Black children. It appeared, at times, that she was determined to single-handedly transform our education and therefore transform our lives. She challenged us, she pushed us, and propelled us forward. She was an educator, a womanist, an activist, and a true fighter for the liberation of Black students in the Chicago Public Schools. In addition to being a teacher, she was also a mentor, a cheerleader, a protector, and sometimes a disciplinarian. She was also a bold, often loud, frank, and painfully honest African American woman from Texas. Mrs. White was never "well-behaved" and was sometimes considered "outrageous, audacious" and "willful" by others. She "spoke her mind" about the conditions of Black people. Even more important, she fought to improve the conditions of Black students in our school. She spoke—even when she was asked not to do so—on our behalf. She demanded the best from her students while continually reminding us how important it was for us to honor our history as Black people and endeavor to be excellent at all times. She continually challenged the White male principal of our school because it was her belief that he didn't "give a damn" about bright Black students like me because we were Black. She pushed him to do more. It was always clear to me that she was absolutely committed to the health and "wholeness" of her Black students even if it meant that she might suffer as a result. As one of her students, I always got the impression that she cared deeply for us—though I cannot recall that she ever said it, instead she lived it and she illustrated it so clearly that it was simply a truth made evident by her actions. Her outspoken activism scared her "well-behaved" colleagues and even led some of them to refer to her as "crazy." She had little concern for what others thought about her. She simply did not care. In fact, she relished in the idea that some were frightened by her brashness.

I met Mrs. White when I joined the beginning choir at Senn High School—then referred to as Senn Metropolitan Academy. Senn was a 45-minute train ride from my house. I ended up there because it was a better option than my local high school: Wells. Wells was riddled with gangs, drugs, and all the other problems associated with large Chicago schools with a history of academic failure. Senn High School was not a high achieving school. But it wasn't a failing school either. It was known for having strong emphases in the arts, science, and technology. Even more important, gangs did not run the place. It was Mrs. Williams—my 5th-grade teacher, also African American, who told my mother she should enroll me there. At Senn, Mrs. Powell, also an African American educator, who was a good friend of Mrs. Williams—looked after me—even though we didn't have much contact. I'd see Mrs. Powell in the hallway and she'd give me the, "I'm watching you, boy" stare. I was never intimidated by her because I could see the look of concern and care in her eyes. I didn't know it at the time, but I'm sure Mrs. Powell shared regular reports on my progress with Mrs. Williams.

At Senn High School, I excelled. I was in the Top 20 during my freshman year. I was in mostly honors classes and joined the National Honor Society and the student council. I was delighted at the opportunities I had to participate in extra-curricular activities including chorus. My elementary school—which was a K–8 school—offered very limited opportunities for extracurricular activities. I had been singing all of my life in the church. I had even performed with *The Soul Children of Chicago*—a professional gospel group. We produced an album that was being played on radio and TV stations all over the world. I had the privilege of traveling all over the region performing. I maintained a fairly grueling scheduling on the weekends performing with this group during my first year of high school. That continued until I met Mrs. White.

During my sophomore year, I joined the high school chorus at Senn. It would be the first time I had ever been taught music in school. Almost immediately, Mrs. White, who was our chorus teacher, took me under her wing. She noted that I had solo ability and began working with me so that I could sing in different languages. The first classical song I learned was "Caro Mio Ben" which means "my dear beloved." It is a late 16th-century Italian love song. It was a simple and fairly repetitive piece from the standard art song repertoire. It was also a good piece for a beginner. We would rehearse during the lunch hour or during breaks. She recommended that I engage in formal vocal study. I had no such experience. She arranged for me to take lessons with a well-respected voice teacher at the Merit Music Program—a grant-funded music preparatory program for city youth. I was able to take lessons and participate in a choral group at no cost. Mr. Halfvorson taught the choral group and Mrs. Halfvorson was my voice teacher. They were parents to Eric Halfvorson—a famous operatic bass-baritone—who was singing all over the world. I also began singing in the All-City High School Chorus. Young people who participated in the city chorus were considered the best singers from their high school. I was proud to represent Senn and to sing in this group with other top singers from around the city. I also competed in vocal competitions on a regular basis. In addition, Mrs. White took the chorus to various places around the city to perform. I had plenty of solo opportunities. I also sang solos at school for special occasions. When Mayor Harold Washington died, I was asked to sing a solo for the school assembly. Mrs. White had selected me to do so. Suffice it to say, I was famous at Senn. While I was no longer ranked in the Top 20 of class at Senn, I continued to perform well academically.

In 1987, Mrs. White nominated me to participate in the Golden Apple Foundation's newly minted scholarship program. This new initiative—funded by local White venture capitalists—was a spin-off of a program they developed to honor top educators across the city of Chicago called the Golden Apple Teachers program. The program was highly regarded. They decided to launch their first group of Golden Apple scholars in 1989. The scholars had to be young people who had chosen teaching as their professional path. In addition to completing an application, one had to also participate in an interview. Dozens of young people applied for the prestigious award. I was selected along with 14 other high school juniors from across the city. We would receive financial support, along with mentoring, and a summer job working in various settings working with children. I was interviewed by the *New York Times* and *CNN*. I went to DePaul University in Chicago on a music scholarship. I later changed my major to elementary education.

The Golden Apple Scholars program made it possible for me to get valuable experience in classrooms while earning needed income in the summers while I was in college. By the time I graduated from college, I was well-prepared for the classroom. I also got academic enrichment in the summers with Golden Apple. One of my summer instructors who taught in the Golden Apple Scholars program was Bill Ayers. At the time, I was not aware that Bill was an internationally recognized education scholar who had written several books on teaching. As I neared the end of my college experience, he recommended that I go to graduate school. I had been mentored by another African woman educator—Dr. Vera Rhimes (mother of Shonda Rhimes) who was trying to steer me toward Dartmouth College in New Hampshire. As a child of the city, I was not certain that I would not enjoy living in New Hampshire. To Dr. Rhimes' dismay, I never applied to Dartmouth. Instead, I applied to Columbia University's Teachers College at the direction of Bill Ayers. At the time, I did not realize that Columbia University was an Ivy League institution and that the degree would open up opportunities for me that I never imagined possible. At some point, Bill did tell me that. But I didn't understand it until I experienced it. All of this happened because of Mrs. White who recommended me for the Golden Apple Scholars program where I met Bill Ayers.

Mrs. White's insistence that I reached beyond my own dreams for myself, helped to propel my career as an education scholar and leader. I also had a strong personal connection to her. I recall that when I graduated from college and later with my doctorate, she was there. She would always say, "I've got to go and see about my Marvin, honey!" When I moved back to Chicago with my growing family to teach at the University of Illinois at Chicago, Mrs. White was there for all of us. She invited us over for dinner and helped acclimate me to the Black middle class on the southside of Chicago. I grew up poor in Chicago. So, I had little association with that community. As I discovered, because Black-middle-classness is not just about how much money you make or how many degrees you have, it's very much about your lineage—who your people are. My people, at least on my mother's side, are mostly poor folk. As a tenured professor working at a major university in the city with a doctorate from a world-class university, I was expected to be part of the world—I think. But I felt like an outsider, an interloper, someone who didn't deserve to behold the titles and the prestige that came with being a tenured university professor at a major research university. Mrs. White disrupted those feelings for me. She helped me focus my energy on a key community transformation initiative. Mrs. White and I soon collaborated on an effort to bring opera to the south side of Chicago and we developed South Shore Opera Company of Chicago in collaboration with the Chicago Park District. The South Shore Cultural Center became the home of this fledgling but important community-based artistic effort. She worked tirelessly to help make the company a success. We celebrated, to great fanfare, our immensely successful opening in the Winter of 2009. A year later, my dear Mrs. White was gone. She discovered she had a brain tumor and left this earth no less than 6 months later. I was not prepared for this. She was close to 90 years old at the time. It didn't matter. I grieved hard. In fact, I still do. Perhaps it is an expression of my deep gratitude to her for having the courage, the tenacity, the passion, and the commitment to care enough to invest in my development. She exemplified the qualities of the womanist educators in Henry's book who were angry about how schools treated the children they referred to as their own. Like Mrs. White, they took action to correct the problems they knew their students encountered. Even more important, she gave of herself, her time and even her resources to support us even into adulthood. Mrs. White will forever be emblazoned in my heart.

IMPLICATIONS FOR POLICY AND PRACTICE

My success as an educator, a scholar, and leader is due, for the most part, to my teachers. My life's mission has been to tell stories about teachers who were like my own and then work to help teacher education programs produce more teachers like the ones I had. Mission impossible? At times. But I persist. Over the last 2 decades, I've learned a few things about what must happen at the state, university, and college/school level in order for this to occur on a large scale. First, states must have explicit policy that prioritizes the recruitment, retention, and advancement of teachers of color. In order to do this, the state legislature must fund scholarships and other forms of support for candidates of color. In addition, they can incentivize school districts to partner with communities of color and institutions of higher education to advance "grow your own programs" (Gist, Bianco, & Lynn, 2018). Universities too must place particular emphasis on workforce diversity as a key goal. It is not sufficient for a school or college to take up this issue without the support and backing of the institution. Presidents, provosts, and deans must be in alignment on this matter. In addition, workforce diversity efforts must be buttressed and lifted up by broader institutional goals that value equity, diversity, and inclusion and see workforce diversity efforts as a key manifestation of these larger goals.

Teacher education programs must have an explicit commitment to advancing teacher diversity while also ensuring that teacher candidates become proficient in culturally sustaining practices that recognize historic inequalities and attend to their students' intellectual, socio-emotional, linguistic, and cultural needs. In order to do this, they must be in partnership with school districts and with communities. We must break down traditional barriers between institutions of higher education (particularly elite, research-focused ones) and the communities in which they sit. Institutions of higher education must have explicit "engagement" agendas that include a commitment to advancing workforce diversity across all of their schools and colleges. Deans, department chairs, and faculty must be willing to roll up their sleeves and work alongside troubled school districts to be part of the solution. Many of us have the ability to write grants that bring much needed resources to support these agendas. We must include our school district partners in these efforts. Finally, institutions of higher education must work to diversify the full-time faculty—both tenure and non-tenure track. Faculty of color are far more likely to lead and invest deeply in efforts to recruit, retain, and successfully produce teachers of color who will have a strong commitment to teaching in urban schools with diverse populations.

REFERENCES

Cannon, K. G. (1996). *Katie's cannon: Womanism and the soul of the Black community.* New York, NY: Continuum.

Gist, C. D., Bianco, M., & Lynn, M. (2019). Examining grow your own programs across the teacher development continuum: Mining research on teachers of color and nontraditional educator pipelines. *Journal of Teacher Education, 70*(1), 13–25.

Henry, A. (1998). *Taking back control: African Canadian women teachers' lives and practice.* Albany: State University of New York Press.

CHAPTER 10

MUSIC EDUCATION AS A VEHICLE TO DREAM, EMPOWER, EXPLORE, AND INSPIRE

The Life and Legacy of Mrs. Arcelia Simmons

Brian L. McGowan

Heritage high to thee we sing, a joyous song of praise
Love and respect integrity, we will remember thee always
Ring those bells on Heritage campus, sing those songs like never before
Maroon and silver thy colors be, you will always remain a part of me
Truth and knowledge is thy soul, a place where everyone excels we're told
Thy fame will forever be sealed by faith and loyalty
Heritage high our pride and joy, we honor thee forever more

—Heritage High School Alma Mater

Once you enter Heritage High School (HHS) through the main doors, take a few steps, make the first left, walk through the doors, go down the hall until you see the vending machines, and make a quick right. Mrs. Simmons'

The Impact of Classroom Practices, pages 93–104

office is the first office next to the vending machines on the music wing. Depending on the time of day, odds are that one of the following three things were happening: (a) you heard choral tones with a great balance, rich tone quality, and good blend; (b) you heard Mrs. Simmons teaching students how to read music; or (c) you heard Mrs. Simmons giving students a meaningful lesson about life. Once inside, you noticed three rooms in the back of the classroom, a piano approximately two feet from the chalkboard, and a group of chairs in an oval shape in front of the piano. This was what I now call my magic space. One that provided you room to dream beyond your circumstances, one that empowered you to develop your leadership skills, one that allowed you to explore your passions, and one that inspired your confidence and gave you a sense of hope. Mrs. Simmons created a transformative educational space that fostered excellence. She embodies characteristics that align with the aims of this text and I am honored to write a story about how she impacted both my teaching practice and life.

I begin this chapter by providing insight into four salient influences in Mrs. Simmons' educational and life trajectory. Next, I draw on culturally responsive teaching and pedagogy literature as a lens to situate this story. Then, I reflect on critical moments I recall while at HHS regarding her pedagogical techniques and behaviors. I then describe how she impacted my teaching practice. I end this chapter with recommendations for teacher education.

MRS. SIMMONS AND FOUR SALIENT INFLUENCES ON HER EDUCATIONAL AND LIFE TRAJECTORY

Mrs. Arcelia Simmons, a native of Palmer Park, Maryland was the inaugural chorus teacher at the "new magnet school" located in downtown Newport News, Virginia in 1996. A graduate of Norfolk State University, she has devoted her career to empowering young educators to pursue their dreams despite their life circumstances. She exudes confidence and drive and seeks to instill these qualities into her students. She often found herself being the first in many contexts, including the first Black person ever to be in her high schools' top musical ensemble. To truly know Mrs. Simmons is to understand the four important influences that shape her educational and life trajectory. These include her family, faith, HBCU experiences, and a Black woman music educator in Greenbelt, Maryland. I describe each of these influences below.

Family

Mrs. Simmons' parents were working-class. They instilled in her a strong work ethic and to not use excuses as a reason to not get things done. She was aware of the racism that her parents endured but they persevered and remained resilient. For Mrs. Simmons' parents, success was not about how much money you made; but more about how you managed what you had. These were lessons that Mrs. Simmons embraced, and instilled into her students. She embraced a family first mindset. She is a wife with a supportive husband, three daughters, and a son. She often discussed the importance of family and shared stories about her children in class.

Faith

A long-term member, choir director, and musician of New Life Church in Hampton, Virginia, Mrs. Simmons often discussed her faith and the ways it shaped her life. She is a giver. During a discouraging time early in her teaching career, she heard a word from God that has carried her over the years. God told her, "As you pour into somebody's child, I will pour into yours." She draws on the Matthew 10:8 bible verse, "Freely you have received, freely you give." She has poured into and cared for thousands of students and believes her own children are successful due to her enactment of this message. All of her children have completed bachelor's degrees in music with some having masters' degrees.

Historically Black Colleges and Universities Experiences

Attending Historically Black Colleges and Universities (HBCUs) impacted her outlook on life and racial identity. Mrs. Simmons initially attended South Carolina State University (SCSU) but transferred and graduated from Norfolk State University (NSU). Prior to attending SCSU, she possessed some anti-Black attitudes based on negative examples that she observed in her hometown and viewing her Black peers' classroom misbehavior as a barrier to her own learning as the teacher was oftentimes unable to teach. After being denied admission to the University of Maryland College Park where they told her that she was "not a good enough musician," she attended SCSU. Her experience at SCSU instilled in her a sense of Black pride. She witnessed her Black peers having a strong desire to learn. This attitude for learning resonated with her and she felt comfortable in this new setting. She often talked about the relationships she built at NSU as being life changing as well.

Dr. Barbara Baker

Mrs. Simmons knew by the third grade that she would be a music teacher. Having experienced both good teaching and observing others who could not maintain control of their classrooms motivated her to be a caring and committed teacher. Dr. Barbara Baker was the chorus teacher at the rival nearby new tech magnet school Eleanor Roosevelt High. She did not get a chance to talk to Dr. Baker at the time but seeing her conduct a choir changed her life. For Mrs. Simmons, witnessing a Black woman on the podium was new to her and this representation mattered. Mrs. Simmons aspired to be like Dr. Baker and had a full circle moment when she met her 27 years later where she conveyed to Dr. Baker that her poise, confidence, and presence changed her life.

In the ensuing section, I theorize about race and culturally responsive approaches that Mrs. Simmons' drew on in her teaching practice. Although Mrs. Simmons may not have had these specific theories in mind, I appreciate how her behaviors and commitments aligned with culturally responsive teaching and pedagogical approaches.

CULTURALLY RESPONSIVE TEACHING AND PEDAGOGY

Culturally responsive pedagogy (CRP) has been linked to positive outcomes for ethnically diverse students in schools across multiple educational phases including high school environments. CRP is defined as using the cultural characteristics, experiences, and perspectives of ethnically diverse students as conduits for teaching them more effectively (Gay, 2018). CRP assumes that when academic knowledge and skills are situated within the lived experiences and frames of reference of students, they are more personally meaningful, have higher interest appeal, and are learned more easily and thoroughly (Gay, 2002). According to Gay (2018) culturally responsive pedagogy encompasses four teacher pillars of practice and eight student outcomes. These pillars of practice (caring teacher attitudes/expectations, culturally diverse content in the curriculum, cultural communication in the classroom, and culturally congruent instructional strategies) describe the critical aspects of a culturally responsive teacher. The eight student outcomes (validating, comprehensive, multidimensional, empowering, emancipatory, transformative, humanistic, and normative and ethical) characterize teaching approaches that work best to support ethnically diverse students.

- *Caring teacher attitudes.* Culturally responsive caring teachers care *for* and actively work to ensure the personal well-being and academic success of ethnically diverse students in their classrooms (Gay, 2018). Caring teachers recognize the children in their classrooms as both students and as people. Consequently, this type of caring results in teachers treating their students in humane ways, holding them in high regard, having high expectations, and employing strategies that support students in achieving these expectations (Gay, 2018).

- *Culturally diverse content in the curriculum.* Curriculum content is a tool that supports students in emphasizing their capabilities, attitudes, and experiences (Gay, 2018). Teachers that make knowledge accessible and connected to the lives and experiences outside of school empower ethnically diverse students.
- *Cultural communication in the classroom.* Communication, culture, teaching, and learning are codependent. Culture strongly influences communication styles among students from different ethnic groups. Teachers that understand how to effectively communicate with ethnically diverse students can impact their academic success.

This chapter, highlights Mrs. Simmons, a culturally responsive teacher, and her ethic of care, communication skills, and integration of Black content in the curriculum. My interactions with her are recounted below.

RECOLLECTIONS OF ACADEMIC SUCCESS DURING MY HIGH SCHOOL YEARS

Mrs. Simmons' classroom was my magic space. It was an incubator to create dreams. I felt safe in her classroom and oftentimes did not want to leave. I knew that I could talk to her about anything and she helped me through many personal situations primarily around issues of poverty in my hometown. I was taught at an early age that despite facing adverse circumstances, education was the ticket to a fulfilling life. She encouraged me to focus on the things that I could control. We had fun learning music. Mrs. Simmons made us laugh just by being herself. I remember the occasional hitting of the wrong note on the piano or not being able to sing certain notes when teaching the soprano or bass sections followed by the words, "You know what I mean." She even gave students rides home after concerts or late rehearsals if they did not have transportation. I signed up for an extra choir class a few semesters just to have more time in my magic space. Her ability to get the most out of her students is what made her stand out from other teachers. Mrs. Simmons provided exposure to Black composers, access to opportunities in music, and showed tough love while teaching confidence. These were traits that I vividly remember from my high school years and I briefly describe them below.

Exposure to Black Composers and Appreciating Black Voices

In *The Dreamkeepers: Successful Teachers of African American Children*, Ladson-Billings (2009) stated that culturally relevant teaching allows Black students to be academically excellent while still being able to identify with Black culture. Mrs. Simmons' actions encouraged this type of excellence among her students. She connected music content to real world events and our home communities. Further, given how choral music education is often approached from a Eurocentric perspective, she deliberately exposed us to music arranged by Black people in addition to teaching some of the commonly taught Eurocentric pieces. I remember singing songs arranged by Black people such as *Every Time I Feel the Spirit* (William Dawson), and *Joyful, Joyful* (Mervyn Warren). I also remember other songs arranged by those who were not Black. These included jazz numbers *A Nightingale Sang in Berkeley Square* (Gene Puerling) and *Pennies from Heaven* (Kirby Shaw) and classical pieces *Cantique de Jean Racine* (Gabriel Fauré) and *Regina coeli* (Wolfgang Amadeus Mozart).

In addition to exposing us to a wide array of music genres, she taught us to embrace the uniqueness of our voices as Black singers. Our choirs were predominantly Black, and she spent time shaping our tone and blend. I remember this vividly when practicing for my district and state choir auditions. She told us that we had to be twice as good and would often say, "Do it again," to make sure we learned our voice parts and represented ourselves in the best possible manner. I made the all-district choir 4 consecutive years and finished first runner up for all-state my junior year. You could only audition for all-state your junior and senior years. I recall auditioning for a solo in Swahili at the district level and ended up getting the part. While learning this song, she employed a critical lens and encouraged me to explore what the song was about. She wanted me to learn the meaning behind the song.

Exposing Students to New Experiences and Access to Opportunities

Mrs. Simmons was adamant about exposing her students to life opportunities beyond my hometown and saw music education as a way to do so. She believed that completing high school and getting the first generation of Black children into college would inspire and increase the chances for others to follow. If students did not desire to attend college, she encouraged them to be a productive member of our society. She made us feel like we had worth past high school and that we could accomplish anything.

My family was proud that Mrs. Simmons created opportunities for us to expand our horizons. First, I went to Florida my freshman year and performed at a highly selective music festival that featured choirs from across the country. We also auditioned and were selected to perform at the White House during their winter holiday series. Some of the guys in the top choirs at my high school and I formed a music group and performed songs throughout the Hampton Roads area. These experiences allowed me to grow as an artist and taught me how to dream beyond my immediate circumstances. Mrs. Simmons also created an environment where her current and future students felt like they belonged. Lastly, I recall Black alumni from the first two HHS graduating classes coming back to visit and discuss their experiences being music majors at Old Dominion University (ODU). We even had an ODU student complete their student teaching at HHS. These experiences shaped my college selection process. I knew that I wanted to follow in their footsteps and chose to attend ODU to major in music education. Talk about a full circle moment, while at ODU, I visited the HHS choirs and completed one of my required internships under Mrs. Simmons' supervision.

Showing Tough Love and Teaching Confidence

Mrs. Simmons employed a tough love approach and did not accept excuses. She pushed us even harder if she felt like we were making excuses. As one of the first freshman ever selected to the top choir at HHS, I was often nervous when singing in front of my upperclassmen peers. Mrs. Simmons taught me to not make excuses even at times when I messed up. For me, her tough love approach was familiar and reminiscent of a Black grandmother giving you the stern but loving look. As a Black woman teaching Black students, many of Mrs. Simmons actions were familiar and positively resonated with me and my peers. When students misbehaved, Mrs. Simmons would give you a look and you knew what it meant. The look was sometimes accompanied with an eraser or piece of chalk in her hand. I was well-behaved in high school but do recall getting the look once. This look was also given when she felt like one of her students was not living up to their potential, which could have been a result of them lacking confidence.

I recall a conversation with Mrs. Simmons about teaching confidence. For Mrs. Simmons, teaching confidence was key to tapping into a student's potential. She was cognizant of the challenges posed when her students did not possess confidence. For instance, she mentioned that children from backgrounds similar to mine sometimes internalize not being good enough when all they need is for someone to believe in them and understand their talent. I also remember the manner in which she selected soloists and it was not always based on who had the best voice. She picked the person who wanted to learn. She picked the person who she wanted to build confidence. I also recall the day she found out that I had perfect pitch. She pushed keys on the piano and would test if I could name the key. I became our choir's pitch pipe whenever we needed to find our starting note. I was nervous but she instilled confidence in me even on the rare occasion where I was sharp or flat.

Mrs. Simmons instilled in me several lessons while I was at HHS. Exposing us to a wide array of music arrangers, particularly Black ones, helped me to appreciate different genres of music and validated my singing voice. Exposing us to opportunities to leave our hometown was inspirational and it taught me how to dream. Her tough love approach and desire to teach confidence has carried over into my own teaching philosophy. In the next section, I discuss the ways in which Mrs. Simmons impacted my approach to the classroom and teaching practice.

MRS. SIMMONS IMPACT ON MY TEACHING PRACTICE

After completing a Bachelor of Music in music education from ODU, I switched professions and pursued a career in higher education. For the past 15 years, I have been an administrator in university housing and residence life, a researcher in a higher education center focused on student engagement, and a full-time faculty member in higher education and student affairs programs. In addition to drawing on the lessons that I observed from Mrs. Simmons during my HHS years, I reflect on three ways that she has influenced my teaching practice. I learned about the importance and responsibility of being a Black teacher, the need to employ a challenge and support approach, and the creation of a fun and supportive learning environment. I briefly discuss each of these below.

The Importance and Responsibility of Being a Black Teacher

All of my professional experiences have been at traditionally White universities where Black professors are sorely underrepresented. Given this unfortunate reality, I understand the importance of being a Black professor as students are not accustomed to seeing us on these campuses. I deliberately promote critical thinking and often pose "how" and "why" questions for students to understand the origins of and rationale for their perspectives. This is similar to when Mrs. Simmons made me understand what I was singing about when learning music. Mrs. Simmons was a storyteller who told stories about her HBCU experiences and choir memories. She instilled in me and my peers a sense of pride about being Black and introduced us to some of the sociocultural realities that Black people face. Similarly, I convey stories that connect students to course content, make broader connections to societal systemic issues, and deliberately incorporate Black authors and guest speakers in my courses.

Challenging Students and Offering Support in the Learning Process

In graduate school, I remember learning about Nevitt Sanford's (1968) theory of challenge and support. Sanford indicated that for student development to occur, the environment must balance the challenge and support offered to students. The optimal goal is to give students an appropriate amount of challenge and provide adequate support. I learned this concept from Mrs. Simmons' tough love approach way before I learned Sanford's theory. She had high expectations but gave us the tools to meet them. I operate from the same paradigm. My teaching philosophy is reflective of my commitment to social justice and change that can transpire through education and co-constructed learning environments. I strive to establish a learning environment that is supportive and promotes risk-taking by students. I do not accept mediocrity. I set high expectations while providing students' tools to meet them in the learning process.

Creating a Fun and Positive Learning Environment

Mrs. Simmons created a learning environment that was fun and positive, and I recount her showing aspects of her personality that were engaging and funny. We laughed often. Whether hitting wrong notes or telling stories that prompted laughter, I remember getting so much out of her classes. I knew that she cared about me as a person beyond my ability to sing or read music. I strive to do the same with my students and bring aspects of myself into the classroom setting to foster a co-constructed fun learning environment. We share and celebrate accomplishments with one another to create a supportive environment. I rely on popular culture and use music to emphasize course content. Further, I design activities where students can be creative and bring their culture and positionalities into the assignments. Lastly, you will often find me being in tune with what my students are feeling while in class because it is difficult to teach when they are not mentally present. Mrs. Simmons checked in on me and I regularly do check-ins with my students before or after class. Inspired by the life and legacy of

Mrs. Simmons, a culturally responsive music teacher, recommendations for teacher educators are presented below.

RECOMMENDATIONS FOR PRACTICE

Magic Space: Integrating the Contributions of Black People Into the Curriculum

Mrs. Simmons transformed her classroom into a magical space where students saw individuals (Black composers) who resembled them in the curriculum. The integration of the contributions of Blacks in the P–16 curriculum has been a topic of interest across all content areas. Extant literature has documented how the inclusion of Blacks into the curriculum positively impacts the preparation of pre-service teachers to teach and support ethnically diverse students (Atwater, Freeman, Butler, & Draper-Morris, 2010; Butler, 2014). Research has also suggested that the exclusion of the experiences of minoritized populations in the curriculum render their experiences as not valued, promotes White inferiority, and fosters prejudice in classrooms (Souto-Manning, Llerena, Martell, Maguire, & Arce-Boardman, 2018). Mrs. Simmons supplemented her music curriculum by including Black composers in her lessons. Teachers need to first be cognizant that curriculum may be "culturally irrelevant" before actively finding ways to transform their curriculum so that students from majority and minoritized populations have an accurate understanding of the contributions of all populations in their disciplines. Teacher educators should supplement their curriculum with perspectives of individuals who have been omitted from the mainstream literature. Furthermore, professional development for in-service teachers (ISTs) must include workshops that can support ISTs in helping students make better cultural connections between their positionalities and the curriculum.

Fostering Excellence: Holding High Expectations Creates Educational Opportunities

Mrs. Simmons had both high expectations and a high regard for her students. Her high expectations created a space that was void of excuses and fostered excellence. She challenged students and offered adequate support to help them accomplish their goals. Her high expectations also encompassed exposing students to experiences and providing them opportunities (i.e., White House performance), which allowed them to be academically successful. Exposing students from marginalized populations to multiple (in-school and out of school) experiences has been linked to increasing student's pursuit of career aspirations and matriculation in post-secondary environments (Russell & Atwater, 2005; Watkins, 2016). Teachers that hold high expectations of their students create positive atmospheres for them to succeed. Subsequently, students internalize these feelings and believe they are capable and act accordingly. Teachers need to recognize that their views of students can negatively or positively impact their students' academic success and must constantly engage in self-reflection to ensure they are always holding high expectations of their students. Teacher education programs must introduce teacher candidates to theoretical frameworks that provide pre-service teachers (PSTs) the necessary lenses to better navigate their classroom spaces and support their student's growth. In addition, including theoretical perspectives like Sanford's (1968) theory of challenge and support in training for both PSTs and ISTs can be helpful as they create their lesson plans, assessments, and classroom spaces to support all students.

Representation Matters: Impact of Black Teachers on Black Students

Ladson-Billings (2009) highlights the importance of Black students having Black teachers in their educational journey. Highly trained Black teachers are critical to the academic achievement of students in classroom spaces and beyond. Mrs. Simmons was a caring teacher who deemed teaching confidence as essential to unlocking a student's potential. Caring has also been found to be a trait of Black teachers that positively resonates with Black students (Geelan, Mensah, Rahm, & Maulucci, 2010). Mrs. Simmons was a source of support for me in high school and an exemplar of a Black, caring teacher who positively influenced my teaching practice as a college professor. Simply put, the representation of Black teachers matters. Teacher educators and school district leaders need to recognize the importance of preparing highly qualified Black teachers to support the academic success of Black students and actively commit to increasing the recruitment and retention of Black teachers.

CONCLUSION

My aim in this chapter was to highlight Mrs. Simmons, a powerful Black music teacher, and the ways she inspired and empowered me as a student at HHS in Newport News, Virginia. Mrs. Simmons is a culturally responsive teacher who created a magic space that positively contributed to the success of students in her music program. More broadly this chapter provides insights into the profile of a culturally responsive teacher and serves as a guide for teacher educators to support the preparation and development of numerous Mrs. Simmons' across all disciplines. Doing so will allow students from diverse and disadvantaged backgrounds opportunities to excel, dream, and achieve success in the classroom and beyond.

REFERENCES

Atwater, M. M., Freeman, T. B., Butler, M. B., & Draper-Morris, J. (2010). A case study of science teacher candidates' understandings and actions related to the culturally responsive teaching of 'Other' students. *International Journal of Environmental & Science Education, 5*(3), 287–318.

Butler, M. (2014). Second-class citizens, first-class scientists: Using sociocultural perspectives to highlight the successes and challenges of African American scientists during the Jim Crow Era. In M. M. Atwater, M. L. Russell, & M. B. Butler (Eds.), *Multicultural science education: Preparing teachers for equity and social justice* (pp. 29–40). New York, NY: Springer.

Gay, G. (2002). Preparing for culturally responsive teaching. *Journal of Teacher Education, 53*(2), 106–116.

Gay, G. (2018). *Culturally responsive teaching: Theory, research, and practice* (3rd ed.). New York, NY: Teachers College Press.

Geelan, D., Mensah, F. M., Rahm, J., & Maulucci, M. R. (2010). Roles, caring and learning to teach science. *Cultural Studies of Science Education, 5*(3), 649–663.

Ladson-Billings, G. (2009). *The dreamkeepers: Successful teachers of African American children* (2nd ed.). San Francisco, CA: Jossey-Bass.

Russell, M., & Atwater, M. (2005). Traveling the road to success: A discourse on persistence throughout the science pipeline with African American students at a predominantly White institution. *Journal of Research in Science Teaching, 42*(6), 691–715.

Sanford, N. (1968). *Where colleges fail: A study of the student as a person.* San Francisco, CA: Jossey-Bass.

Souto-Manning, M., Llerena, C., Martell, J., Maguire, A., & Arce-Boardman, A. (2018). *No more culturally irrelevant teaching (Not this but that).* Portsmouth, NH: Heinemann.

Watkins, S. E. (2016). *African American male PhD scientists and engineers: Perceptions of factors that impact their persistence in STEM through a lens of critical race theory* (Unpublished doctoral dissertation). University of Delaware, Newark, DE.

CHAPTER 11

MENTOR TEACHERS' IMPACT ON EDUCATOR IDENTITY AND RACIAL LITERACY DEVELOPMENT

Yolanda Sealey-Ruiz and Lum Fube

Mentorship has long been a means by which individuals aspiring toward a particular goal, whether professional or personal, could obtain counsel from a person who previously achieved that milestone. Though there is no exact consensus on the definition of mentoring because it is frequently conflated with advising, numerous scholars have described the roles of mentors and benefits to mentees or protégées (Darwin, 2000; Griffin, 2012; Hansman, 2001), namely providing career and psychosocial support as one works towards a goal. Though traditional mentoring relationships within higher education may lead to desirable outcomes for students, mentors receive little to no reward for their service. Acknowledging that mentoring is a cultural activity, mentoring models developed to support Black female doctoral students and faculty—what Darwin (2000) situated within the radically humanistic perspective—are mutually beneficial and operate within

The Impact of Classroom Practices, pages 105–116

a framework of collective achievement. This approach differs dramatically from a mantra of survival of the fittest that exists within traditional mentoring models. Instead, this approach reflects what Molm (as cited in Griffin, 2012) identified as generalized exchange and mutual dependence relationships. Similarly, mutual dependence relationships are marked by indirect reciprocity but with a goal of collective success attached to a social justice agenda. Though not directly benefiting from these types of mentoring relationships, some faculty express feelings of satisfaction knowing that they have contributed to developing the next generation of scholars committed to social justice issues and culturally responsive research (Griffin, 2012; Pallas, 2001; Tillman, 2001).

In this essay, Yolanda (a tenured associate professor at an R1 university) and Lum (a doctoral student at the same R1 university) reflect on the mentoring they received during their educational journeys. They recognize how the mentoring they received—Yolanda, from a Black woman, and Lum from a Black male—helped them break through silence, awaken their social consciousness, and discover that their position as Black women in academic institutions required a particular type of mentoring to help them understand and navigate their experiences, develop their research voice and agenda, and ultimately remain on the path of their academic trajectory.

As Lum's story reveals, it is possible for Black women to navigate academic settings successfully within a cross-racial mentoring relationship (Griffin, 2012; Tillman, 2001). Work by Jackson, Sealey-Ruiz, and Watson (2014) show the strengths of mentoring youth across gender through an ethos of care and reciprocal love. Yolanda's story affirms that Black female dyads are particularly successful because of the mentor's ability to understand and relate to the ways in which the intersection of race and gender influences their experiences in academia (Collins, 2000; Grant, 2012; Hu, Thomas, & Lance, 2008). A study conducted by Johnson-Bailey, Lasker-Scott, and Sealey-Ruiz (2015) showed that mentoring relationships developed between Black women revealed particular ways in which they read their experiences. In what they call *the gendered literacies of mentoring*, their study revealed that a Black woman's social position in American society forces them to experience life, and thus their life experiences in predominantly White institutions, in ways that are vastly different from other women. Their study showed that within the culture of individualism and "publish-or-perish" reflected in academe, mentoring relationships grounded in Black Feminist Thought (Collins, 2000) supports the collective ideas of achievement that Black female faculty desire and require to succeed.

LUM'S STORY

The ever-present reality of abiding in multiple cultural spaces as an undergraduate student sent me running toward a sense of trying to understand where I belonged. This quest started during my senior year of high school. I ran for and was elected student council president. When the gavel was handed to me during the inaugural ceremony, the teacher announced I was the first African American to become president in the history of the school. In my head, I corrected him. I was the first *African* to become student council president. I often made this correction in my head.

One of our student council projects involved collecting books and donating them to the local library. We successfully organized and collected books for the book drive. Another student council member and I were tasked with delivering the books to the local library down the street. He loaded most of the books in his car and the remaining books in my car. I arrived at the library first and told the attendant at the help desk I was from our local high school to deliver books from our book drive. She told me to drive around to the loading area and another attendant would help me unload the books. I drove around to the other side of the library and waited for the attendant. As I saw the doors begin to open, I climbed out of my vehicle and walked towards the woman to introduce myself. The startled, surprised, and confused look on her face caused me to slow down and approach her with bewilderment. As I came closer, she frowned and crossed her arms. I introduced myself and said I was the student council president who was dropping off the donations from our book drive. Her arms remained folded and she looked me up and down. She stood there in silence.

A few moments later, my classmate, a White male student, pulled up in his pick-up truck and walked over to my car. He looked at my face and saw the confusion in my eyes. Opening the door to the backseat of my car, he stacked some books in his arms and walked over to the entrance. He introduced himself to the attendant, in an almost verbatim greeting. This time, she smiled and exclaimed, "Of course!" and directed him where to put the books. I stood there in shock as he continued to unload the remaining books in my car.

Awakening Consciousness

The awakening of consciousness around racial literacy (Guinier, 2004; Sealey-Ruiz, 2011; Singleton, 2014; Twine, 2003) was a slow and gradual process for me. The vignette I shared above was the beginning of this awakening, but my understanding of what had unfolded would take years to unpack. My track coach in high school, Mr. Gholston, would be an integral part of my awakening, but I would not come to appreciate the lessons he taught me until many years later. Attending a predominantly White high school often meant Black students and their experiences existed on the margins (Archer-Banks & Behar-Horenstein, 2011; Ispa-Landa & Conwell, 2015; Murphy & Zirkel, 2015; Posey-Maddox, 2017). Mr. Gholston made it a point to educate us on the Black excellence we were being deprived of in our schools. He organized enrichment field trips and programs for the Black students. He especially went out of his way to advocate for Black students when it came to disciplinary matters.

Although Mr. Gholston extended himself to provide alternative narratives and histories of Black people, I often felt I could not relate to many of them because they were very much situated in the U.S. context. The histories and narratives I was familiar with were situated *back home.* I longed to read stories by African authors, and during my undergraduate studies, I nourished this hunger. My fixation with African literature and narratives would bring me full circle to understanding African American history. I started studying the transatlantic slave trade and moved on to reading slave narratives and the narratives of Native Americans. If I had been born in a different place and time, I could have been one of the women sold into slavery. This perspective radically transformed how I read and interacted with slave narratives. I could have been *Celia, the Slave.* I visualized myself as Dona in *Kindred* and felt the whips on my body. I cried. At this precise moment, I remembered the silence and the look of disgust the woman gave me at the entrance of the library loading dock, and for the first time, I understood what had transpired. I was being treated as I was because I am Black.

A few years after graduating college, I visited Mr. Gholston and unearthed memories from my high school days. He asked me if I remembered the time I told him someone in my family said Black Americans are lazy. I looked at him with pure embarrassment and shock. He laughed and said I was young at the time and recently immigrated. He understood that was something my family and people told me, and he also remembered schooling with Africans and hearing similar things. I also shared many ignorant and hurtful comments I heard about Africans from other African Americans. In that moment, sitting and drinking coffee with Mr. Gholston, I realized the lessons he had tried to teach me through many field trips and enrichment programs. First, contrary to the colorblind approach taken by my predominantly White high school, racism existed and would be imposed on me, whether I identified as African or African American—and regardless of how many times I corrected them in my head. Second, Mr. Gholston was pushing me to question the assumptions I was taught about Black Americans by exposing me to what I had come to see as Black excellence and Black girl magic.

What I appreciated most about Mr. Gholston was his pedagogy of love. He did not get upset or berate me if I said an ignorant comment. He set out to teach me something different and allowed me to counter the narratives I had been taught, thus beginning the journey of challenging my assumptions and undoing my internalized racism.

YOLANDA'S STORY

Mahatma Gandhi once said, "In a gentle way you can shape the world." I have always viewed the mentoring I received from Dr. Suzanne Carothers, my first and only Black female professor during my doctoral studies at New York University (NYU), as her gentle way of helping to shape the world. Even now, 15 years after completing my doctoral degree, I remain grateful for the mentorship I received from Suzanne. Suzanne saw her mentoring as a service—to her doctoral students and to the world. It was her way of leaving the world (of academia) a better place than how she found it, through the students she guided along their educational journeys. I have so many memories of the way Suzanne mentored my Black female colleagues and me while we were in graduate school at NYU, but one particular event stands out in my memory—one that shifted the way I saw myself as a doctoral student and deeply impacted my trajectory as a scholar.

I distinctly remember the day. It was at the beginning of the spring semester during the second year of my doctoral program at NYU. I remember that the class had been a particularly tense one that day. My two best friends (Carmen Kynard and Avon Connell) and I were taking the doctoral seminar with Suzanne and four other professors. During class, there had been a heated debate about the intersection of race and class and how it perniciously played out in most urban public schools across the country for Black and Brown children. New to the concept of debate using the research I read in my classes, I just became angry and outwardly upset about what I felt were uninformed comments made by the White students. They seemed to speak with so much assurance about Black and Brown communities that they had never lived in or visited. In my anger, I lashed out in class. Carmen, who had much more experience in responding to these types of comments in an academic way, jumped into the conversation and began citing scholars to help the students clearly see their racist remarks. Avon just rolled her eyes in disgust and shut down from the conversation.

When the seminar was over, Suzanne made eye contact with the three of us from across the room. We were huddled in the back of the room talking about what had just happened in class. She wanted us to join her in her office. We left the classroom and followed her down the hall.

We entered her office, one behind the other, like ducklings following their mother duck across a pond. I sat across from Suzanne in a black chair that swiveled from side to side. I was nervous and moved side to side in the chair as I thought about how I had let my impulsive nature get the best of me and "showed my hand" in class. Carmen and Avon sat still in the stationary chairs also across from Suzanne. All eyes were on Suzanne. She leaned forward, looked at the three of us, smiled, and asked, "So how do you think that went?" We were silent, until I impulsively jumped in. "What do you mean?" I asked. "You mean the class?"

She nodded. It was clear she was referring to how I became angry, Carmen stood passionately and firmly in her refusal to have racist comments made in our presence, and Avon shut down. Suzanne asked another question: "What do you think could have been done differently?" Again, out of my nervousness, I jumped at the opportunity to answer her question.

"Maybe I didn't have to get so angry. Yeah, I guess I could have reacted differently."

Suzanne smiled at us. There we were, the only three Black women in our cohort, and our Black female professor. Suzanne was one of two Black women professors in our entire academic department. As the only three Black females in our cohort, Carmen, Avon, and I had become accustomed to hearing our White peers make racist, erroneous, and hurtful statements about children who looked like us, lived in communities similar to ours, or reflected the lives of the students we taught every day. Suzanne, who was *my first and only* Black female professor, wanted to help each of us understand the context we were in, the "nature" of the academy, and why it was important to understand it was not our job to protest every racist statement that came out of the mouths of our White classmates. That day she reminded us that we had the right to engage in the doctoral process as students, and not *just* as defenders of our race. She helped us to remember that we were admitted to NYU because we were smart and belonged there, and that we did not have to prove anything to our White peers or anyone else about our shared communities. We deserved to experience the doctoral journey just as they did—we had that privilege and we should use it. I remember leaving her office feeling both relieved and enlightened. I often felt that way whenever I left a mentoring session with Suzanne. Her mentoring that day changed the way I interacted with my White peers in the program moving forward. It also led me to take a specific interest in how to facilitate constructive conversations about race and racism in the classroom. In a very significant way, Suzanne led me to my path of becoming a scholar of racial literacy.

Suzanne was the only Black woman teacher I ever had—from elementary school throughout my college experience. I had been taught by a few Black male teachers along my academic journey, but *never* a Black woman. Having now acquired academic language for my experiences, I know that I would have suffered even more severely from racial battle fatigue (Smith, 2004) in my doctoral program (and later in my journey to tenure) had it not been for Suzanne's mentoring of me. Now that I am a tenured faculty member at a predominantly White institution, very similar to my alma mater, I have become that same teacher to my students of color that Suzanne Carothers was to me. Suzanne remains a significant presence in my life, and up until my tenure at Teachers College a few years ago, I relied on her sage advice for navigating a space where I often felt marginalized. Throughout my tenure journey, I often recall that day at NYU as well as other incidents where I learned from Suzanne's wisdom—wisdom that led me to focusing my current research agenda on race.

Why I Study Race

Specifically, I study the impact of race and racism on the lives of students and teachers. I write about my findings through the lens of racial literacy development. I began to study race to help me understand my experience as a Black woman in racist America, and specifically how it affects Black and Brown people in schools. The concept of race is deeply rooted in our lives and articulated through our legal system and schools; it affects how we think, speak, and perform culture. Ruth Frankenberg (1993) noted that race, like gender, is "real" in that it has real, tangible, and complex impact on individuals' sense of self, experiences, and life chances. Developing the racial literacy of educators is critical to helping them succeed in school and read the racialized world in which they live. If educators are able to engage in these critical conversations, then they are better equipped to resist the accepted racist practices that their students of color endure in their school settings and in society. If my racial literacy had begun to develop while I was a student at NYU, perhaps I would have responded differently that day in the doctoral seminar. If my teacher education program had been focused on developing the racial literacy of its students (and faculty), perhaps the conversations involving race in my seminars and other courses would have been more constructive and productive.

Racial literacy in teacher education, for example, can go against the ways that colleges and universities perpetuate the status quo of White supremacy through curriculum that normalizes Whiteness and discourages open and critical conversation about race (Churchill, 1995; Schick, 2002). Racial literacy in teacher education calls for self-reflection and moral, political, and cultural decisions about how teachers can be catalysts for societal change—first by learning about systems of injustice and then explicitly teaching their students what they have learned through the use of dialogue, critical texts, journaling—all means of helping to develop their critical thinking and conversation skills around the topics of racism, discrimination, and prejudice. Last, racial literacy asks that teachers take action against injustice in their school settings once they recognize it. Three tenets guide the individual's journey into becoming racially literate: question assumptions, engage in critical conversations, and practice reflexivity. In education writ large, and teacher education specifically, there is limited theorizing around racial literacy development (Johnson, 2009; Rogers & Mosley, 2006; Skerrett, 2011). Studying racial literacy not only helps me understand the power of my mentoring experience with Suzanne, but also helps to shape the way I mentor my students today. My co-author and I recognize how our mentoring relationships led us to see our experiences with Mr. Gholston and Suzanne Carothers as a way to develop our own racial literacy. This has been a lasting strength of our mentoring relationships, and in my case has specifically led me to become a scholar of racial literacy. In the next few paragraphs of this essay, we briefly discuss aspects of racial literacy as a way to illuminate the growth we experienced about our own understanding of race during our mentoring relationships.

DEVELOPING RACIAL LITERACY

Racial literacy is a concept developed by sociologist and feminist researcher France Winndance Twine (2003). Twine's research in the United Kingdom with English and Irish women who were members of interracial families (parents of children fathered by Black men) revealed a form of racial socialization in which these parents engaged to protect and defend their children against racism. Racism is a structural phenomenon that determines one's status and opportunity in society based on skin color and the ascribed racial category to which they belong. Racism is the belief that one race is superior over another. In the case of American racism, this belief is supported by the legal system and practiced through acts of discrimination against as well as prejudice and antagonism toward other races. It is codified through societal and cultural practices. Twine (2003) advanced the notion that racial literacy is enacted through strategies and practices that are linked to culture and heritage. This approach requires that one must respond to acts of racial injustice (in action and words) with action and words in order to counter racism. What Twine found significant in her research on countering racism for African-descendant children was the use of aesthetic and material resources that promote the intelligence, creativity, and significance of the culture of Black people across the Diaspora, including in the United States.

Racial literacy is a skill and practice in which individuals are able to probe the existence of racism and examine the effects of race and institutionalized systems on their experiences and representation in U.S. society (Rogers & Mosley, 2006; Sealey-Ruiz, 2011; Skerrett, 2011). A desired outcome of racial literacy in an outwardly racist society like America is for members of the dominant racial category to adopt an antiracist stance and for persons of color to resist a victim stance. Racially literate students reflect on their experiences with race and are reflexive about their attitudes and beliefs. They read texts that are meant to elucidate their understanding of race and racism and equip them with language to talk about these two concepts. The ever-increasing diversity of our classrooms and our world makes a strong case for racial literacy education. The concept of racial literacy is informed by scholarship that recognizes race as a signifier that is discursively constructed through language (Hall, 1997); fluid, unstable, and socially constructed (Omi & Winant, 1986) rather than static; and not rooted in biology, but as Frankenberg (1996) wrote, having "real" effects in the lives of individuals.

RACIAL LITERACY AND MENTORING IN TEACHER EDUCATION PROGRAMS

As witnessed in both our stories, teachers have varied and storied lives, which influences their understanding of their context and surroundings. We encourage preservice and in-service teacher preparation programs or institutions to create spaces for ongoing interrogation of the self in relation to the institutions and communities of which we find ourselves a part. This interrogation involves learning and understanding the historical, sociopolitical, and cultural contexts, as well as our social positions and systems of power and oppression that come with our ascribed social positions. Being aware of the many selves that live within us awakens a critical consciousness and awareness of our intersecting identities and the ways we see ourselves as the oppressed and oppressors. Racist teacher assumptions that remain unchallenged can have harmful implications for the communities the teacher serves because the teacher may continue to view the community unconsciously from a deficit lens. The tenets of racial literacy highlight how we were mentored by Mr. Gholston and Suzanne Carothers, and offer implications for ways teacher education programs can engage their students and faculty toward a more open environment for conversations on race, racism, and education. The teaching and practice of questioning assumptions, engaging in critical conversations, and practicing reflexivity can serve as a practical approach for mentoring as well as helping to develop the racial literacy of students and faculty in the academy.

Fundamental to racial literacy development is for individuals to question their assumptions about race, acknowledge their biases, and take the stance that much of what they "assume to know" about race is faulty and incomplete. In questioning assumptions about race, individuals can actively resist and interrupt the racist and discriminatory practices, policies, and beliefs they encounter in their teaching sites. Engaging in critical conversations is an integral component of racial literacy development. Individuals must be encouraged to, and eventually develop, the confidence to discuss their hesitancies and concerns about teaching in racially diverse settings. The intent of these critical conversations is to focus on language and how biases and racist attitudes are articulated, sometimes in an unconscious or dysconscious manner. Critical conversations are outlets to question assumptions that individuals hold about race actively and openly. Reflexivity in racial literacy development is a cyclical process of (re)examining perceptions, beliefs, and actions relating to race. It is a crucial step in racial literacy development. This promotes the idea of (de)constructing and (re)building a base for new perceptions founded on open-mindedness and a more informed understanding of how race operates in academic spaces.

REFERENCES

Archer-Banks, D. A. M., & Behar-Horenstein, L. S. (2011). Ogbu revisited: Unpacking high-achieving African American girls' high school experiences. *Urban Education, 47*(1), 198–223.

Churchill, W. (Ed.). (1995). White studies: The intellectual imperialism of U.S. higher education. In *Since predator came: Notes from the struggle for American Indian liberation* (pp. 45–64). Littleton, CO: AIGIS.

Collins, P. H. (2000). *Black feminist thought: Knowledge, consciousness and the politics of empowerment.* London, England: Routledge.

Darwin, A. (2000). Critical reflections on mentoring in work settings. *Adult Education Quarterly, 50*(3), 197–211. https://doi.org/10.1177/07417130022087008

Frankenberg, R. (1993). *White women, race matters: The social construction of Whiteness.* Minneapolis: University of Minnesota Press.

Grant, C. M. (2012). Advancing our legacy: A black feminist perspective on the significance of mentoring for African-American women in educational leadership. *International Journal of Qualitative Studies in Education, 25*(1), 101–117. https://doi.org/10.1080/09518398.2011.647719

Griffin, K. A. (2012). Black professors managing mentorship: Implications of applying social exchange frameworks to analyses of student interactions and their influence on scholarly productivity. *Teachers College Record, 114*(5), 1–37.

Guinier, L. (2004). From racial liberalism to racial literacy: *Brown v. Board of Education* and the interest-divergence dilemma. *Journal of American History, 91*(1), 92–118.

Hall, S. (1997). *Race, the floating signifier.* Northampton, MA: Media Education Foundation. Retrieved from http://www.mediaed.org/cgi-bin/commerce.cgi?preadd=action&key

Hansman, C. C. (2001). Who plans? Who participates? Critically examining mentoring programs. In *Proceedings of the 42nd annual adult education research conference* (pp. 161–166). East Lansing: Michigan State University.

Hu, C., Thomas, K., & Lance, C. (2008). Intentions to initiate mentoring relationships: Understanding the impact of race, proactivity, feelings of deprivation, and relationship roles. *The Journal of Social Psychology, 148*(2), 727–744.

Ispa-Landa, S., & Conwell, J. (2015). "Once you go to a White school, you kind of adapt": Black adolescents and the racial classification of schools. *Sociology of Education, 88*(1), 1–19.

Jackson, I., Sealey-Ruiz, Y., & Watson, W. (2014). Reciprocal love: Mentoring Black and Latino males through an ethos of care. *Urban Education, 49*(4), 394–417.

Johnson, M. T. (2009). *Race(ing) around in rhetoric and composition circles: Racial literacy as the way out* (Unpublished doctoral dissertation). The University of North Carolina at Greensboro, Greensboro, NC.

Johnson-Bailey, J., Lasker-Scott, T., & Sealey-Ruiz, Y. (2015). *Mentoring while Black and female: The gendered literacy phenomenon of Black women mentors.* Manhattan: Kansas State University Press.

Murphy, M. C., & Zirkel, S. (2015). Race and belonging in school: How anticipated and experienced belonging affect choice, persistence, and performance. *Teachers College Record, 117*(12), 1–40.

Omi, M., & Winant, H. (1986). *Racial formation in the United States: From the 1960s to the 1980s.* New York, NY: Routledge.

Pallas, A. M. (2001). Preparing education doctoral students for epistemological diversity. *Educational Researcher, 30*(5), 6–11. https://doi.org/10.3102/0013189x030005006

Posey-Maddox, L. (2017). Race in place: Black parents, family–school relations, and multispatial microaggressions in a predominantly White suburb. *Teachers College Record, 119*(1), 1–42.

Rogers, R., & Mosley, M. (2006). Racial literacy in a second-grade classroom: Critical race theory, whiteness studies, and literacy research. *Reading Research Quarterly, 41*(4), 462–495.

Schick, C. (2002). Keeping the ivory tower white: Discourses of racial domination. In S. H. Razack (Ed.), *Race, space, and the law: Unmapping a White settler society* (pp. 99–119). Toronto, Canada: Between the Lines.

Sealey-Ruiz, Y. (2011). Learning to write and talk about race: Developing racial literacy in a college English classroom. *English Quarterly: Journal of the Canadian Council of Teachers of English Language Arts, 42*(1), 24–42.

Singleton, G. (2015). *Courageous conversations about race: A field guide for achieving equity in schools.* Thousand Oaks, CA: Corwin Press.

Skerrett, A. (2011). English teachers' racial literacy knowledge and practice. *Race, Ethnicity and Education, 14*(43), 313–330.

Smith, W. A. (2004). Black faculty coping with racial battle fatigue: The campus racial climate in a post-Civil Rights Era. In D. Cleveland (Ed.), *A long way to go: Conversations about race by African American faculty and graduate students* (pp. 171–190). New York, NY: Peter Lang.

Tillman, L. C. (2001). Mentoring African American faculty in predominantly white institutions. *Research in Higher Education, 42*(3), 295–325.

Twine, F. W. (2003). Racial literacy in Britain: Antiracist projects, Black children and White parents. *Contours: A Journal of the African Diaspora, 1,* 129–153.

CHAPTER 12

A RETROSPECTIVE NARRATIVE ON EFFECTIVE TEACHING AFTER MOVING FROM SEGREGATED TO INTEGRATED SCHOOLS

Implications for Policy and Practice on Effective Teaching

Zollie Stevenson, Jr.

Narrative inquiry and autoethnography in research are being utilized as a research strategy to collect more authentic research on different cultures particularly in education settings (Trahar, 2009). A premise of narrative inquiry is that human beings find meaning in their lives through the stories that they tell (Andrews, Squire, & Tambokou, 2008). Related to the qualitative research approaches of interpretive hermeneutics and phenomenology, narrative inquiry is the form of research that uses written, oral, and visual narratives that focus on the meaning people give to their experiences

The Impact of Classroom Practices, pages 117–126

which can then be used to understand the complex interactions of our lives. Riessman and Speedy (2007) offered the following definition for the term narrative:

> The term narrative carries many meanings and is used in a variety of ways by different disciplines, often synonymously with story... the narrative (pays) analytic attention to how the facts got assembled that way. For whom was the story constructed, how was it made and for what purpose? What cultural discourse does is draw on-take for granted? What does it accomplish?" (pp. 428–429)

Personal scholarly narratives aid in the exploration and understanding of knowledge *from* the past and not necessarily knowledge *about* the past from those who share their stories (Bochner, 2007).

My retrospective story focuses on elementary and secondary school teachers whom I perceived as effective has enabled me to reflect on my educational experiences and the efforts and strategies that I believe were effective in enabling me to engage with my teachers and to learn, as well as to develop an enthusiasm for the activities that promote learning. My elementary school experience began in racially segregated schools in rural Guilford County, North Carolina where I was taught by Black teachers exclusively. Rena Bullock School, located in southeastern Guilford County, contained Grades 1–9 during my enrollment and I attended Grades 1–3 there (Buchanan, 2001). When my parents separated, my siblings and I moved with our mother first to Greensboro, where I attended Mt. Zion Elementary School, and later to a Rosenwald school, Brown Summit, in northeastern Guilford County (Brown Summit, n.d.).

All my teachers during those years were African American and mostly female. The only male teacher that I had during Grades 1–8 was while in 7th and 8th grades at Brown Summit, Mr. Melvin Charles Smith. Mr. Smith provided structure and discipline in class. He was a no-nonsense teacher who engaged us with his sense of humor as well as his teaching. He was always well dressed and often connected with us by sharing stories of his own children and their schooling and home experiences. He was known for using a ruler to discipline students when they were off task or unruly. He was a gifted trumpet player, becoming a well-known jazz musician in the community. Having a master's degree from NC A&T State, as his family grew, he left Brown Summit to become the first African American Chief Federal Probation officer in the state of North Carolina. For a young Black male who lived in a household with his mother and who would only see his own college educated father every other weekend, Mr. Smith engaged me in learning but also served as a positive model of an educated, talented, and stable Black man during a time of upheaval in my young life (Wells-Wilbon & Holland, 2001).

I also received nurturance and reinforcement of my strong oral reading skills and reading comprehension from my third-grade teacher Mrs. Verta Mae Allen at Rena Bullock and my sixth-grade teacher Mrs. Louise Faucette at Brown Summit (Finnian, 2009). Mrs. Allen allowed me to assist with classroom chores and gave me a sense of responsibility and she always permitted me to be one of the readers during oral reading time. She was warm and grandmotherly and loved to have students read aloud in class. Mrs. Faucette was a wonderful formal lady and great teacher who used a lot of music and films to enhance learning and engage students. I was one of two students in her class who was permitted to operate the Chapter 1 (later Title I) film projector to show the various historical and science films that the school purchased using federal funds. Fat and clumsy as I was then in my hand-me-down clothes, I also was selected by Mrs. Faucette for speaking roles when our class was responsible for hosting one of the school assemblies and for special programs. Even after leaving Brown Summit, I kept in touch with Mrs. Faucette through my high school years and would be invited for cookies and iced tea at her home in Greensboro.

In 1967, the school districts in Guilford County began to implement desegregation plans as a result of the *Brown v. Board of Education* (1954) Supreme Court decision. It took 13 years for school districts in North Carolina to take steps to comply with the courts binding ruling. To prepare for the transition from segregated to integrated schools, Grades 9–12 were removed from Brown Summit and students in those grades had to transition to formerly all White Northeast Guilford High School. As my class was promoted from seventh to eighth grade, Brown Summit instituted a new instructional model where we changed classes for the first time among four teachers. We were being prepared to enroll at the new Northeast Junior High School which was going to receive ninth graders from formerly predominantly White and predominantly Black elementary and reconfigured schools in northeastern Guilford County.

While the changes were being made in the schools, crosses were being burned in the yards of Black students in our neighborhood who had chosen to attend the predominantly White Northeast High School before the high school grades at Brown Summit were eliminated. Gunshots were also being fired at the homes of Black students who chose to integrate Northeast High School. So, there was fear among Black students and their families as the transition plans moved forward.

Our eighth-grade teachers, Mrs. Lillie Alston (mathematics), Mr. Smith (who moved with us from seventh to eighth and taught social studies), and teachers such as Mrs. Faucette, worked with the students to allay our fears and to teach us some of the strategies such as using our “educated” words instead of curse words and fists if we encountered any negative interactions when we moved to the newly integrated junior high school.

When the time arrived for us to move to Northeast Junior High as 9th graders, we rode on segregated buses to the school looking very different and with an air of nervousness. We did not know what to really expect in terms of interactions and even if we would be smart enough to compete with the White students at the school. I remember that I put extra Royal Crown in my hair and wore a stocking cap to change the look and texture of my hair. Others conked their hair and the girls mostly wore pressed hair starting off. We wore our new and best clothes and wanted to appear equal to the White students that we would meet in classes. Most of the faculty were White, but we felt fortunate to have Mrs. Alston, the mathematics teacher from Brown Summit on faculty at Northeast. The librarian from Brown Summit also landed a position as librarian at the junior high school. They were the only familiar faculty and staff persons. The faculty was overwhelmingly White. Busing was the means for moving us from our homes to Brown Summit and from Brown Summit to Northeast which was another 30 minutes further than the busses that took us to Brown Summit which added to the length of the day.

We were received in class at Northeast without any drama by most of the faculty, though I noticed that occasionally the raised hands of Black students to respond to questions asked by White teachers in some classes were ignored on a regular basis. Civics was my strongest class and I remember that I often knew more than most of the students in the class, but I was overlooked when I raised my hand and if a White student did not answer correctly a question that I knew the answer to, rather than call on me, the teacher would provide the correct answer. I remember being reprimanded by the teacher when, frustrated, I blurted out the correct answer to questions when none of the other students responded to her questions. There were clearly favorites in most of my classes and none were Black. We made it through the year with a few fist fights and protests because of the selection of all White cheerleader squads for sports teams that were composed mostly of Black males. There were no sports teams for females in junior high school. Children notice these things.

Towards the end of my ninth grade year, my parents reconciled. They bought a house in Greensboro, and so for my 10th grade year, we moved from the country to the city, and I attended Walter Hines Page High School in Greensboro. Page and Grimsley High Schools were the preeminent predominantly White high schools in the city at that time. The school attendance area for my working-class neighborhood in northeast Greensboro was rezoned along with Black middle and upper class Benbow Park neighborhood from southeast Greensboro to increase the Black presence at Page High School. This was the period when "freedom of choice" was also a part of the integration process used to determine where students attended school. Page had tracks and I was placed in college prep courses.

Mrs. Lillie Alston moved from Northeast Junior High to Page High School and I was fortunate to have her for Algebra I after a poor start with a White teacher who mostly socialized with the White students in class and ignored the Black students.

Schools in North Carolina were still adjusting to integration and thus the few Black teachers on faculty were attempting to fit it just as Black students were trying to adjust. Some of the Black students had attended junior high school with some of the White students and had become friends. This was particularly true among the guys who played football or basketball. Most of the Black students were enrolled in business/vocational education classes where in some classes they outnumbered the White students. I noticed after a short period during my 10th grade year that there was some tension between the Black students in college prep classes and those in business/vocational education classes. I noticed that some Black students enrolled in business/vocational education classes who lived in my neighborhood stopped speaking to me and occasionally tried to instigate fights with me and others in college prep, and I learned that some college prep students stopped associating with Black students in business/vocational education classes. This dynamic continued throughout the 3 years of high school with the only disruption of this pattern occurring when issues that frustrated both the Black college prep as well as the business/vocational education students brought us together... items such as the absence of Black cheerleaders on the varsity or junior varsity squads; the failure of faculty to select or students to elect Black students for the homecoming court; the absence of Black presence on student council; or to be elected to senior class superlatives. Black students were present but not necessarily considered a part of the school, so it seemed.

I also noticed that differences were being made by some Black students in terms of their families perceived social standing within the college prep student track. There were a few middle- and upper-class Black students who did not interact with the working-class Black college prep students outside of class, even in the cafeteria. This situation did improve over the 3 years. No administrator, teacher, or counselor (Black or White), attempted to build bridges between or within the various student group configurations. I believe as I think back that the same divide existed for White students in the college prep and business/vocational tracks, but at the time I was not focused on their experiences.

At Page High School, I felt connected in the classroom with Miss Sue Ellen Medley (10th grade English); Mrs. Margaret Garrett (Advanced Composition); Mr. Dwight Bartlett (U.S. History); Mrs. Lillie Alston (Algebra I); Mrs. Winifred Woodruff (World History); and Mrs. Lorraine Gail (career counselor). Each expressed an interest in the work that I completed for class and provided helpful and considerate feedback that helped me to improve my performance. They were kind and inclusive of all the students in their classrooms. We did a lot of writing in the English classes taught by Miss Medley and Mrs. Garrett. Miss Medley was very approachable and while Mrs. Garrett very traditional and reserved, she was an excellent and detailed teacher and made no difference in the students in our class. Because of Mrs. Alston, I learned to love Algebra I and II and did well in those classes. The history teachers, Mr. Bartlett and Mrs. Woodruff were engaging teachers of that subject, especially Mrs. Woodruff. All those teachers, except Mrs. Alston, were White. It was in those college prep courses that I began to actualize my belief that I was going to go to college and that I was college material.

It was in high school that learning and the desire to know more really hit me. That spark was ignited by Mrs. Winifred Woodruff who taught World History. Not only did she engage me in the classroom, she also influenced my career interest in teaching, research, and scholarship. Winifred Woodruff, in her manner and style would remind most of us of the quintessential history teacher lost in the history books and texts as well as her memories of actual visits to the sites where Revolutionary and Civil War battles and other significant historical sites. She and her husband spent summers taking train trips and learning deeply about history, beyond what was covered in sanitized textbooks, and they traveled the world developing a deeper understanding of this information. A middle aged White woman with salt and pepper hair with a cropped cut, she had this wonderful bang covering part of her forehead that she would flip or toss back as she elucidated details on an event in world history, hands emphasizing the particular point that she was making. She wore huge glasses which made her eyes seem even larger when she was expressively sharing details, her eyes growing larger as she elucidated on the topic. I was so engaged by her in the classroom that I religiously read my World History text and I would sit with her during study hall or at the end of the class day to learn more. She gave me additional information to read so that I developed a deeper understanding. It was Mrs. Woodruff's class that I was first exposed to African history via a student teacher who was assigned to her. Mrs. Woodruff helped me to understand that the voluminous world history book that we were using in class did not contain all the facts or context associated with history. That knowledge helped me understand that part of what had not been shared in the World History textbook was valid and important context of history and that exploration and reading would help me to be able to know the context of history and other content as well if I explored more deeply. It was via Mrs. Woodruff that I really began to read books that focused on African history and literature, using the city libraries to learn more. By the time I reached my senior year, I was determined that I would attend college and become a history teacher, just like Mrs. Woodruff.

CONCLUSION

I have been engaged by many but not all teachers in my elementary and secondary experience. I felt motivated to learn by those teachers who made the effort to get to know me and to learn the strategies that motivated me to engage with the learning process. I felt nurtured, cared about and valued by Mrs. Allen, Mrs. Faucette, Mr. Smith, and Mrs. Alston, Black teachers all, during the days of segregation. At Page High School, connections with teachers mostly seemed to evolve around the content that they were teaching in which I had an interest (i.e., social studies/history), felt challenged (English composition and creative writing) or with whom I felt a connection (the Algebra I teacher who seemed to relocate as I moved from Brown Summit to Northeast Guilford to Page High School and the career counselor at Page). In particular, the Algebra I teacher and career counselor, African American women, both took an interest in me. It was in those college prep courses that I began to actualize my belief that I was going to go to college and that I was college material... despite the comment by my White high school guidance counselor that I was not college material. (I ultimately did my internship for the master's degree in counseling and though not assigned to her, got to work collaboratively with that guidance counselor 5 years after she disparaged my ability to get into or be successful in college.) The final section will highlight some recommendations for policy and practice.

RECOMMENDATIONS FOR POLICY AND PRACTICE

The world has changed considerably since my days in a segregated public school setting and transition to an integrated public school setting. Some might say that our public schools have regressed and become more segregated in the 21st century, 65 years since *Brown v. Board of Education,* than they were in the 20th century (Frankenberg, Ee, Ayscue, & Orfield, 2019).

Policy

School Districts Should Establish Policies That Promote Cultural Competence

The intercultural presence in our public schools has increased dramatically since my matriculation in the elementary/secondary system. With the racial/ethnic and language diversity that now exists, it is critical that teachers and school leaders receive training on how to effectively engage students and their family members with an understanding of cultural norms for their racial/ethnic and/or language groups so that children can be effectively engaged in their classrooms and to also engage families in the education of their children. Strategies for preparing teachers to effectively education students of color, particularly African American children, are highlighted in a study and recommended strategies published by Ladson-Billings (2009). Several districts across the county have used Ladson-Billings cultural competence paradigm as a professional development opportunity to enhance the cultural competence of teachers.

Practice

Engage Students in the Learning Process

Teachers who engaged me while I was in elementary and secondary schools, got the best learning results from me as measured by traditional and non-traditional methods. I was attentive in class, I completed homework assignments, I followed directions, I worked well with most of my classmates, and I was not disruptive. Engagement means that The Center for Teaching and Learning at the University of Washington provides information and strategies for engaging students in their learning as well as dealing with classroom management and organization (Center for Teaching and Learning, 2020).

- It is important to engage the students in active learning (projects, hands on activities, working in small groups, use of manipulatives, etc.).
- Use technology to enhance learning using clickers, iPads and other mobile technology, and so on. Develop creative ways to use cell phones as an instructional tool.
- Provide service-learning projects so that students can learn from their experiences and connect those experiences to content provided in class.
- Use in class time for inquiry, application, and assessment rather than traditional lecture and discussion. This approach provides opportunities for students to ask questions of their classmates as well as the teacher. Rather than focus on lectures, assist your students in using Socratic strategies and themes with guided questions to engage student conversations.
- Make connections from the textbook learning to the student experience. Translate the textbook learning materials into activities and discussions that are relevant to student's everyday life.

Develop an Understanding of What Motivates Each Students' Best Efforts in Learning

Each of the teachers who effectively engaged with me observed how I responded to the various instructional strategies, how I related to them as teachers and my classroom was affected to provide opportunities for me to demonstrate my strengths and to work on the areas where I was not as strong in my learning.

- Effective teachers learn to know their students and the skills that those children possess so that they can effectively engage their students (York, 2014).
- Understanding the unique skills and interests of students can aid the teacher in engaging students and incorporating strategies in teaching that will reach all their students.

The policy and practices proposed as a result of my retrospective narrative are huge in scope. With the intercultural diversity that has grown exponentially over the last few decades argues for the effective teacher to be both culturally competent and to have a menu of strategies and approaches that they can employ in public school classrooms to engage students in their learning and to promote high levels of student achievement.

REFERENCES

Andrews, M., Squire, C., & Tamboko, M. (Eds.). (2008). *Doing narrative research.* London, England: SAGE.

Bochner, A. (2007). Notes towards an ethics of memory in autoethnographic inquiry. In N. Denzin & M. Giardina (Eds.), *Ethical futures in qualitative research* (pp. 196–208). Walnut Creek, CA: Left Coast Press.

Brown Summit Middle School. (n.d.). *Our school's history.* Retrieved from https://www.gcsnc.com/domain/20854

Brown v. Board of Education, U.S. National Archives and Records Administration, 1954. Retrieved from https://www.ourdocuments.gov/doc.php?doc=87

Buchanan, B. (2001, December 28). Students recall beloved school: Rena Bullock served Black students in southeast Guilford County in the 1950s and '60s. *Greensboro News and Record.* Retrieved from https://greensboro.com/students-recall-beloved-school-rena-bullock-school-served-black-students-in-southeast-guilford-county-in/article_1c64a614-690e-5b35-98e4-683431488188.html

Center for Teaching and Learning. (2020). *Engaging students in learning.* Retrieved from https://teaching.washington.edu/topics/engaging-students-in-learning/

Finnian, C. (2009) Supporting and nurturing students and teachers in grades 3–6. *Phi Delta Kappan, 90*(6), 400–403.

Frankenberg, J., Ayscue, J. B., & Orfield, G. (2019). *Harming our common future: America's segregated schools 65 years after* Brown. Retrieved from https://www.civilrightsproject.ucla.edu/research/k-12-education/integration-and-diversity/harming-our-common-future-americas-segregated-schools-65-years-after-brown/Brown-65-050919v4-final.pdf

Riessman, C. K., & Speedy, J. (2007). Narrative inquiry in the psychotherapy professions: A critical review. In D. Jean Clandinin (Ed.), *Handbook of narrative inquiry: Mapping a methodology* (pp. 426–456). Thousand Oaks, CA: SAGE.

Wells-Wilbon, R., & Holland, S. (2001). Social learning theory and the influence of male role models on African American children in PROJEECT 2000. *The Qualitative Report*, *6*(4), 1–17.

York, B. (2014). *Know the child: The importance of teachers' knowledge of individual students' skill (KISS).* Retrieved from https://cepa.stanford.edu/content/know-child-importance-teacher-knowledge-individual-students-skills-kiss

CHAPTER 13

"LOVE MANY, TRUST FEW; LEARN TO PADDLE YOUR OWN CANOE"

What Teacher Practitioners Can Learn From Racial Counterstories of a "Master Teacher" in Rural North Carolina

Terrell L. Strayhorn

BACKGROUND TO THE TOPIC

An old proverb says, "A good teacher goes a long way." Working to identify the characteristics and qualities of *good teachers* has been the focus of hundreds of books and studies over the last 50 years or so. For instance, the weight of empirical evidence suggests that effective teachers are loving, supportive, patient, caring, and knowledgeable, to name a few (Foster, 1994). Good teachers, according to research, are joyful, patient, and treat *all students* fairly (Rushton, Morgan, & Richard, 2007). In one study using surveys and essays from 43 students at a prestigious secondary school, good

The Impact of Classroom Practices, pages 127–140

teachers were believed to be good-looking, objective, and skilled in making difficult subjects understandable (Ida, 2017).

Other scholars have emphasized *what good teachers do*. For example, analyzing data from 134 pre-service teachers at a large, southern university in Georgia using sequential mixed methods, one study found that nearly one-third of pre-service teachers believed good teachers were ethical and good class managers, while over half of them emphasized being "student-centered" (Minor, Onwuegbuzie, Witcher, & James, 2002). Relatedly, Ladson-Billings (1995) argued on several occasions that effective teachers employ *culturally relevant pedagogy* in their practice. That is, they draw from the cultural wealth of students' local cultural communities to ensure the academic success, cultural competence, and sociopolitical awareness of students, especially racially diverse learners. She went on to clarify that effective teachers possess the pedagogical and relational dispositions to connect well with students (and their families) in the classroom and beyond. Good teachers employ other-mothering[1] practices (Foster, 1993) that treat all students just like one's own.

Despite reams of studies depicting African American teachers in the South (before and after segregation) as victims of their oppressive environment, equity-minded scholars like Siddle Walker (2001) have used historiography and archival data to *rewrite* the dominant narrative of Black teachers as culturally competent, politically engaged, caring role models. In her pioneering work on the topic, Professor Siddle Walker (2005) has challenged the omission of Black teachers in the larger portrait of public schooling and cast a critical gaze on the ways in which they organized resistance to advocate for better facilities, longer school terms, more transportation, and equitable opportunities for their students.

So whereas we now have considerable evidence about the general qualities and traits of highly effective teachers (Foster, 1993, 1994; Rushton et al., 2007), as well as the habits and ways in which they go *beyond the call of duty* to help their students, we know comparatively less from anecdotes, narratives, and (counter)stories that honor educators, especially Black[2] teachers, who leave an indelible mark on their students, communities, and the greater good. The present chapter is part of a volume intended to fill this critical gap in scholarship.

PURPOSE OF CHAPTER

The purpose of this chapter is to tell the story of a highly effective, public school Black teacher in rural North Carolina whose career provides many lessons from which all teacher practitioners can learn. In this chapter, I will use (counter)storytelling[3] methods, as articulated in critical race theory

(CRT), to paint a racialized portrait that honors and memorializes the professional legacy of Creola Evelyn Warner (my maternal grandmother). The chapter is organized into three major sections. First, I introduce readers to "Miss Warner," as the admirable teacher of focus and identify the characteristics that qualified her for this designation. Then, through counter storytelling, I describe in rich, thick details how she used these qualities in her teaching practice, both inside and outside the classroom, to equip and empower her students. Lastly, I show through words—including interview data from several of her former students—the impact that she made (and continues to make posthumously) on them, her community, and the lives of many others whom she taught. A final section highlights key recommendations for future practice, policy, and pedagogy.

THE LIFE HISTORY OF "MISS WARNER"

Born October 6, 1925 to Snowd Ephraim and Dollie Wilder, Creola Evelyn was one of four children: Urcher, Garvin (aka "Buck"), Creola, and Martha (in birth order). She attended "grade school" in the local community and transferred to Pollocksville High School in 7th grade, where she excelled academically. There was no school in her neighborhood at the time so she and her siblings had to walk "over two miles each way, back and forth to school in the rain, sleet, and snow," if they wanted to learn. "Papa [Ephraim] was OK at first... but he got sick of [them] having to walk so far to school," so he let them stay with his sister who lived in-town (closer to Pollocksville High), from Sunday through Friday until they finished school.

Young Creola loved to learn and she "loved her teacher" who went by the name "Miss Jenkins." She taught in a single-room schoolhouse, teaching students with varying learning styles, different grade levels, and very different abilities, but she "did it all" with no teaching assistant, no assistive technology, and little to no training about differentiated instruction (Alexander & Winne, 2006), multiple intelligences (Gardner, 2000), or self-directed learning styles (Canipe & Brockett, 2005). What she lacked in formal training, Miss Jenkins more than made up for in creativity, commitment, and personal investment in the success of her students, especially Creola. Miss Jenkins attended Elizabeth City State University (ECSU), a historically Black college/university (HBCU), and often encouraged her students, "Get your lesson out, study hard, and you can go as far as you wanna [*sic*] go."

That's exactly what Creola did. She loved to study, and "get her lesson" (i.e., homework) out of the way early, so she could devote most of her discretionary time to helping her mother in the kitchen, looking after her younger sister (Martha), and "picking tobacco out in the backfields," as she would often recount. After graduating high school, she attended ECSU, following in the footsteps of her beloved teacher, earning a bachelor's degree in *Language Arts* with a concentration in elementary education.

With a degree in hand, Creola Evelyn landed her first teaching job in a public school district in the state of Georgia. She taught "reading and writing" to students in "every grade they had at the time," so the story goes. Her teaching skills were recognized quickly by district leaders and she was called upon to work with more novice teachers, offering advice about how to work with "troublesome kids," or those with poor behavior in the classroom. After 5 years of service, she moved back to her hometown and accepted a job at Trenton Elementary School where she taught for many years. Consistent with the times, Miss Warner "taught almost everyone in town," especially all the Black kids, including her own niece (Jackie), another niece (Angie), and, believe it or not, her own daughter (my mother, Linda). "But you'd never know that any of us were related to her because we couldn't call her "Aunt Creola"... we had to call her "Miss Warner" and she treated us just like all the other kids... fair [*sic*], warm, and with love," as Jackie shared with me.

In so many ways, Miss Warner was a "master teacher" based on her years of professional experience, her teaching competence, and her documented effectiveness in teaching students from different backgrounds and varying modalities to excel academically. Upon retiring after 50 years of professional service, Miss Warner was acknowledged as one of the "longest-serving educators in Jones County" North Carolina. The week following her retirement, Miss Warner went back to substitute teaching and continued doing so until her death in 2013. She was a Sunday school teacher, Vacation Bible School instructor, and tutored kids in the neighborhood all the time "for free... she never charged nobody nothing [*sic*]," her sister (Martha) clarified. "She wasn't in it for the money... she never was; she just loved to teach and loved for them [her students] to learn," she continued.

By all accounts, Miss Warner was (and is) a gifted instructor, a highly effective educator, and exemplified the prevailing traits and qualities characteristic of a good teacher. She was fair, imaginative, joyful, patient, student-centered, and held high expectations for all students to succeed. Indeed, a good teacher can "inspire hope, ignite the imagination, and instill a love of learning" (Jan, 2017). That's exactly what she did. The next section uses counter-storytelling methods to demonstrate *how* she did this, both inside and outside the formal classroom.

HOW "MISS WARNER" TAUGHT THEM: A COUNTER-STORY

A Quick Word About Counter-Storytelling

Counter-storytelling emanates from a long line of scholarship arguing for the use of CRT in education research as a way of engaging "a more robust racial analysis" (Cook & Dixson, 2013, p. 1238) in a field (education) where race was once largely under-theorized, according to prominent scholars (Ladson-Billings & Tate, 1995). CRT provides theoretical justification for the use of narrative and (counter)storytelling as legitimate aspects of methodology, methods, and *authentic* ways of knowing. And in keeping with that tradition, I acknowledge that "critical race theory writing and lecturing is characterized by frequent use of the first person, storytelling, narrative, allegory, interdisciplinary treatment of law [and related subjects], and the unapologetic use of creativity" (Bell, 1995, p. 899).

Despite my predominantly positivist leanings in conducting quantitative educational research, I *see myself* as a "quantitative criticalist" (Stage, 2007). I readily recognize the *enormous* power, possibilities, and utility of CRT generally, and counter-storytelling specifically, as a tool for "challeng[ing] dominant narratives by intentionally centering analysis on the marginalized voices" (Cook & Dixson, 2013, p. 1243). In this chapter, those marginalized, *all-too-often* overlooked and silenced voices are the experiences and insights of a Black public school teacher in a rural southern district and her "churrin" [*sic*] (southern dialect for "children"), as she often referred to her students. Contrary to popular and *dominant narrative* beliefs, whether in the classroom, courtroom, cornfield, or churchhouse, "Miss Warner" taught her students using the resources, strategies, and tools necessary to reach them where they were located within a larger social context. Her methods morphed and changed as/when needed, but consistently exemplified the *very best* of what we know from research nowadays about effective, engaging pedagogy. In this way, she was both *before her time* and *of her time*, and her career success *speaks against* the master narrative—"a narrative that is based on the social and cultural history of the dominant race" (Cook & Dixson, 2013, p. 1243). Below, I use counter-storytelling methods to illustrate "*how she taught her churrin' to learn, learn, and keep on learning*...," as her last-living sister shared with me during an interview[4] recounting the teaching career of her "big sis."

Sets Clear, High Expectations for All: "Mind the First Time... and Love Many"

> Now the one thing about Cre' (short for, "Creola") is she was good at making her students *mind the first time* and no matter what they was gonna' learn. She would tell 'em that all the time. You are going to learn. You can learn. You ain't no dumb dummy. Don't let nobody tell you that. You're Black. You're beautiful. And you *can* [emphasis added] learn. Stop saying you can't... oh, she would get so frustrated when they'd say that. "I can't," they say [*sic*]. She'd come back with, "Can kicked can't out" (laughing), that was one of Cre's many mottos seem like. She had a way of making you believe you could do anything. I mean anything, hun (short for "honey"). Conquer the world. Go to the moon and be back by supper (laughing) ... um, um, um, lawd I had me a good sister. I miss my sister, yes I do (shaking her head, fighting back tears). Now she was a teacher's teacher. She could out-teach all them White teachers down there (laughing). They couldn't teach them kids (referring to the White teachers who *moved in* after desegregation). All 'dem kids, like our kids, Cre taught 'em. Must've been thousands or thousands more... she taught 'em all hun. Let me see, she taught Jack (Martha's daughter), Angie, Annie Pearl, Duck, Lin (short for, "Linda")... umm, I can't name 'em all. I mean she taught 'bout every child—Black and White—from here to New Bern, Trenton, Pollocksville, Maysville, all of 'em hun. And the one thing I know they know is my sister believed in them, all of 'em. The White ones *and the Black ones.* "Black ain't got nothing to do with your brain," she'd say. She was strict—they had to mind and *mind the first time.* You know, it's easy to mind the second and third time after you done got [*sic*] in trouble, but looked to me like she was trying to teach them to learn how to *mind the very first time.* She knew it would keep the Black kids safe and alive, especially at that time when they were just looking for any 'ole reason to hit us, or hurt us, or burn us, or something. And she would tell 'em, "The man [i.e., police, White authorities] ain't gonna give you a second chance... you've got to listen and mind the very first time. You hear me?! Say yes, ma'am... yes, sir... have a good day... good morning... speak up and be polite. You can do it! You can be kind to your enemy—treat your neighbor right... that's what the song says (referring to a gospel hymn "Heaven Belongs to You"). *Love many*... love everybody churrin' and you'll live a long life." I think a lot of them thought she was just preaching sometimes (laughing), but Cre' knew what she was doing... she was teaching them how to avoid the man, how to make it out here, and how to stay alive. She'd say all of that in school, Sunday School, Vacation Bible School, it didn't matter. That was one of Cre's big, big things to say... *Love Many*... and she really loved her students. She believed in them. (Martha)

Consistent with everything we know from research about the power of teachers' high expectations on performance of students of color (Gershenson & Papageorge, 2018; Rojas & Liou, 2017), Miss Warner held very high expectations for her students and messaged her endless belief in their potential in many obvious and tacit ways, both inside and outside the classroom. Though situated geographically, racially, and politically within a physical context and broader system that denied Black people's agency (e.g., to vote), questioned their intelligence, threatened their safety, and suffocated their local economies (e.g., tobacco, cotton), Miss Warner *consciously resisted* those oppressive forces, held high expectations for *all students*, shielded her Black churrin' from its decimating blows, and *intentionally* instilled in them, through her teaching and *telling*, Black cultural pride, hope, imagination, and a love for learning, all hallmarks of "a good teacher" (Jan, 2017, p. 51).

Uses Analogy, Metaphor, and Music: "Love Many, Trust Few . . ."

> Rell (short for, "Terrell"), the one thing you got to make sure you tell 'em about Aunt Creola, your grandmother, is she was *one* [emphasis added] smart woman. I'm talking like really smart. Aunt Creola, well, we couldn't call her Aunt Creola at school. Did they already tell you that? (Nodding, I said, "yes") Ok, good. Well, that was 100% true (laughing), she was my Aunt Creola because she married my mother's brother. You follow me? And I could call her Aunt Creola in church, at home, or whenever we went to visit her and Mr. Joyner (her husband). But at school she was "Miss Warner" and that's what we called her. She didn't just teach us academics though. She was my 4th grade teacher. I can't even remember now what you learn in the 4th grade (laughing) but I know Miss Warner taught us *way more* [emphasis] than that. Oh, I remember she would teach us about place values and roman numbers [sic] and how to add numbers with a whole bunch of digits . . . I wasn't really good at that at first (laughing). I would whine and complain, "Miss Warner, I can't . . ." and she would come right back with, "Of course you can't because you keep telling yourself you can't. Can kicked can't out. You can do it. Now try and try hard, even if you gotta' count on your fingers and toes" (laughing). That was always funny to us because we knew Miss Warner knew we didn't have that many toes and fingers, but one thing we know is that she *really cared about us* [emphasis added]. Not just as students, but as kids, as real people who had, you know, a fighting chance to be something in this world. And she was gonna' help us get there by teaching us. Every morning, she would make us sing—it wasn't even music class—but she loved to sing. We'd sing, "Good morning to you, good morning to you, we're all in our places with sun-shining faces; this is the way to start our new day . . ." Look like she knew we needed something to cheer us up early, you know, times weren't easy back then. And she would tell us, "Love many, trust few . . . you can't trust everybody to be your friend, churrin'." She wasn't mean or evil about it, but you could tell what she meant. Trust was earned, not given. You had to build trust by watching what people say and do . . . you don't just go out here throwing your trust away. You ain't gotta' [*sic*] be grumpy and nervous, always looking over your back—nah, she didn't want us to be like that. But she wanted us to be wise and discern-

> ing. She would always tell us a story about an ugly farmer and a pretty worm (laughing). The ugly farmer went out to the field one field and got startled by a pretty worm. The worm pleaded with the farmer, "Please don't kill me, miss farmer, I won't hurt you or your crops. I want to be your pet, winking her pretty little worm eyes." The ugly farmer was tempted to take the pretty worm inside and let it live with her, but then a big red rooster, I think it was, came out of nowhere shouting, "There she is, get her!" The ugly farmer was scared, thinking the rooster was launching an attack against her. Just then, a gang of animals grabbed the pretty worm and yanked its cover off, revealing that it was a *poisonous male snake.* "You can't judge a book by its cover... a snake is a snake, pretty or ugly (laughing)," she'd say. "Love many, love everybody, treat your neighbor right, but trust few... watch out for them pretty, eye-battin' snakes," she'd tell us (laughing). We never knew all the morals to that story, to be honest. It might've been that she wanted the girls to know they could be farmers and leaders, just like boys. Or maybe she wanted the boys to watch out for fast girls. I don't know if any of that was in the curriculum back then, but it should've been [*sic*]. (Vernon)

Another way Miss Warner taught her students "about themselves and the world around them," as one former student put it, was by using associative teaching techniques like analogy, allegory, and metaphor that link events or problems with a relevant context, local examples, or even humor as a way of breeching relatively serious (and sensitive) topics like race, racism, and trust. For instance, Vernon and others recalled how "Miss Warner" taught kids how to multiply numbers by engaging their imagination and knowledge of nearby cornfields—spaces and places with which most of her students were *very familiar*—as a way of helping them to sense and "see" mathematical concepts; associating classroom learning with students' senses has been ranked a powerful recall stimulator (Market, 2001). Countless examples were shared by her former students, like this one, "If you got [*sic*] six rows of corn and five stalks per row, how many stalks do you have total?" she would ask students in private tutoring sessions. "She would be asking questions and waiting for the answer from across the room—we'd be at her dining table working and she'd be in the kitchen cooking her dinner... but she'd still be teaching" (laughing), recalled one former student turned banker.

As an elementary school teacher, Miss Warner covered a range of subjects including math, reading, writing, and more. Former students explained how she taught them to read and write using everyday items. "She would teach us to read, write, and practice our handwriting by making us write out scriptures from the Bible over and over again," another former student shared. "It really didn't matter if your people [family] were churchgoing or not, you were going to learn and the Bible became like a textbook for us... we used to joke, Miss Warner could teach us using anything." Indeed, Miss Warner seemed to specialize in drawing upon local knowledge funds and the community cultural wealth (Yosso, 2006) of her students to make learning "real relevant," as she would often say. She accomplished these learning goals using a mix of methods—analogy, metaphor, music, and parable—all the while encouraging her Black students to fight hate with love, overcome darkness with light, and "trust few" in a way that was still forward-facing, optimistic, and empowering. She did all of this despite earning a college degree in the 1940s long before the cultural congruency movement in curriculum and instruction led to the production of books, articles, and courses on the topic. There's no evidence, from informants, archival records, or her personal belongings at home, that Miss Warner ever read a book or article on culturally relevant pedagogy or analogy-based instruction, yet she practiced it regularly, lived it courageously, and *was it* authentically.

MISS WARNER'S LASTING IMPACT: "LEARN TO PADDLE YOUR OWN CANOE"

Miss Warner "peacefully surrendered her life, answering God's final call" on November 23, 2013, as described in her published obituary. Her long-time pastor, Reverend Sidney Harper, and then-church leader, Reverend Angelo Brown, served as co-officiants. At the request of my family, I delivered my maternal grandmother's eulogy, celebrating her life that mattered *so much* for so many. The printed bulletin read: "Ms. Warner was a consummate teacher, devoting over 50 years of her life to public school teaching. She was a member of Zeta Phi Beta Sorority, Inc., American Legion Ladies Auxiliary, and Trent River Temple of Elk. She was a lifetime member of Freewill Baptist Church, where she taught Sunday school, sang in the choir, and directed the children's choir. Miss Warner will be remembered for her personal motto: 'Love many, trust few; learn to paddle your own canoe.'" Interestingly enough, I wrote, designed, and produced my grandmother's obituary. Once ready, I drove into town (New Bern) to have it printed at Kinko's. Kinko's was right near Hardee's, where my grandmother took me and my siblings for breakfast every weekday morning after swimming lessons. She would walk in, same routine. Half dozen adults would rush around her, proclaiming, "Miss Warner?! Wow, it's so good seeing you." She would look surprised, smirking, and ask, "Honey, do you know me?" They always respond affirmatively, "Yes, Miss Warner, you were my 4th grade teacher." Or, "You were my 5th grade teacher." Or, "You were my 6th grade teacher," reflecting the fact that my grandmother taught many students across most grades in her rural elementary school in Trenton.

I pulled up at Kinko's, overcome with mental images of all the "good times at Hardee's," and walked in to grab copies and be on my way. The desk agent's name was "Alexandra" (I'll never forget it) and I handed her a folder, fighting back tears, and asked for "300 copies... double-sided please." Alex opened the folder and burst into tears, "Miss Warner died... what?!" Shocked, I stood up, looked around, and asked, "Honey, did you know her?" Shaking her head, Alex nodded, "Yes, she was my 4th grade teacher. I'll never forget her. Love many, trust few..." "Learn to paddle your own canoe," we said in unison.

That's the final verse of this counter-story about Miss Warner's *lasting impact* on her students, Black and White, straight and gay, rich and poor. Each and every one of them remembered her life motto and, in several instances, it became their own motto or mantra as well. They interpreted the coda—"learn to paddle your own canoe"—to be her way of teaching them about the importance of self-reliance, self-efficacy, and having "a go-get-em attitude," as one put it. "She would tell us that we can't just sit back and wait for somebody to do it for us... we've got to do things for ourselves," one former student, now charter school teacher shared. She went on to explain:

> That's what she did as a teacher too—we didn't have clubs back then so she created clubs for us and she would make us awards for good behavior by letting us get into groups... well, they were clubs really and we could do stuff together as Black kids, just like the White kids got to do at their schools. She didn't wait for them to give us clubs and stuff, she made 'em up herself. I think that's learning to paddle your own canoe, cuz' most of us didn't even know what a canoe was back then (laughing). So she'd change it up from time-to-time... "Learn to tie your own shoe"... anything 'ole thang [*sic*] that rhymed would work as long as you knew that you've gotta get up and to take responsibility for your own education and never stop learning. That's what I remember about Aunt Creola (laughing), well, Miss Warner. (Jackie)

DISCUSSION

The purpose of this chapter was to tell the story of a highly effective, public school Black teacher in rural North Carolina whose career achievements provide many lessons from which all teacher practitioners can learn. Using critical race theory as a lens and racial counter-storytelling as a method, I describe in *indigenous* detail how Miss Warner enabled the success of all students, especially her Black students, by setting and maintaining high expectations; using analogy, metaphor, and music; as well as nurturing their self-efficacy, intrinsic motivation to learn, and sense of responsibility to "learn to paddle [their] own canoe." Pre-service and inservice teachers can learn a lot from this counter-narrative.

Dozens upon dozens of studies have praised the importance of teachers holding high expectations of their students. High expectations work.

Teachers should check their biases at the door and encourage *all students* to dream, imagine, and stretch beyond their comfort zone. This is particularly important for teachers working with students of color or those from marginalized backgrounds where success is rare or achievement is not often expected (according to dominant norms). Setting high goals, supporting students' growth, and positively reinforcing their performance (e.g., "You can do it," or "Can kicked can't out") are effective strategies for doing so.

We've known that "Black educators are part of the community and [also] part of the schooling structure" (Cook & Dixson, 2013, p. 1238). They are powerfully affected by what happens in both. This is illustrated in Miss Warner's story when institutional racism denies her students access to certain resources (e.g., books, clubs), which would negatively impact her ability to teach as well. Exercising autonomous agency and creative capacity, Miss Warner finds a way to address the problem. Pre-service and inservice teachers today may face similar circumstances due to inequitable school funding formula, unequal local tax bases, and persistent institutional racism that privileges "high-performing" suburban schools while ignoring the social miseries that cripple predominantly minority urban and rural public schools. Teachers remember this: "Circumstances shouldn't matter." Demographics should not determine destiny. That is, where a student is born and grows should not determine their occupation or opportunities, even though a good deal of research shows that is the case. Teachers have the power to intervene. Just like one can feel alone in the midst of millions, creative, committed, compassionate teachers can find wealth in the midst of famine and genius within "goof-offs," so to speak. It starts with high expectations, but it also requires teachers to acknowledge race and racism, expose inequality in systems allegedly as egalitarian as education, and assume the powerful role that they play in either reinforcing or removing inequality through their teaching practices. Culturally relevant pedagogy doesn't have to be complicated or hocus pocus. It's reflected in your examples, texts, videos, language, and rewards. Find ways to incorporate your students' culture and real-life experiences in the classroom. Translate complex topics into simple messages, using their vernacular or terms where possible. Conduct a cultural audit of your teaching materials—who's represented, who's not? What can you do to change it? When in doubt, ask your colleagues, especially colleagues of color, regardless of your own race. Don't be afraid to ask your students too—they can be both consumers and producers of indigenous knowledge.

There are also critical implications for future research based on information presented in this chapter. For example, the chapter itself demonstrates the power and possibilities of using counter-storytelling methods to position a Black teacher in rural North Carolina as a strong advocate for her students, community, and social justice, challenging dominant narratives about Black and/or rural life in America that tend to emphasize poverty, powerlessness, and problems rather than cultural wealth, courageous power, and creative solutions. Paying closer attention to the counter-stories of people of color is important and necessary. Future researchers should also analyze how counter-stories speak back to non-racialized, canonical constructions of Black (and Brown) teachers that typically position them as ordinary, underprepared, and unlicensed (to teach). Making the teacher of color—whether pre-service or in-service—the prominent unit of analysis and telling the story through his/her eyes is one way to (re)write the wrongs in extant literature.

CONCLUSION

I could go on and on with many attempts to connect Miss Warner's story to practical applications for pre-service and inservice teachers. Follow your gut. Realize that everything isn't in a book or conference. Know your students and avoid cookie-cutter approaches that won't work. But, in my intellectual spirit of sorts, I believe *and feel* that I've said enough. Well, actually, the *story itself* has said enough (and more than I may realize) to those engaged in the life-changing, revolutionary act of teaching. Love many. Trust few. Learn to paddle your own canoe. May love and light show us all the way.

NOTES

1. I use the term "othermothering" to reference a long-held tradition of education within Black communities, which according to scholars, acknowledges the nurturing, supportive, kinship-like roles that some Black educators assume when working with students (Strayhorn, 2015).
2. Throughout this chapter, I use the terms "Black" and "African American" interchangeably to refer to people of African descent (e.g., West Indian, Caribbean, Haitian, African) living in the USA.
3. Associated with critical race theory (CRT), counterstory-telling is a methodology or approach to storytelling that posits narratives as credible, crucial, and valued sources of "legitimate knowledge" (Delgado Bernal, 2002, p. 169). Counterstory-telling also "challenges mainstream society's denial of the ongoing significance of race and racism" (Yosso, 2006, p. 10).
4. A quick point about method. The impetus for this project came from my deep, profound love and respect for my maternal grandmother. I've always been enamored by her, her life story, and the many vivid stories she would tell me growing up about her life with "Papa" (Mr. Ephraim), in the 1960s civil rights era, and as a decorated educator. For the purposes of this chapter, I tapped into existing family and professional networks to learn more about the "missing pieces" of my grandmother's narrative. This led to a very purposeful

sampling of informants who were interviewed in homes, coffee shops, family reunions, churches, and by phone, especially since some "information rich cases" (Patton, 2002, p. 230) are well into their 80's and above.

REFERENCES

Alexander, P. A., & Winne, P. H. (2006). *Handbook of educational psychology* (2nd ed.). Mahwah, NJ: Erlbaum.

Bell, D. (1995). Racial realism—After we've gone: Prudent speculations on America in a post-racial epoch. In R. Delgado (Ed.), *Critical race theory: The cutting edge* (pp. 2–8). Philadelphia, PA: Temple University Press.

Canipe, J. B., & Brockett, R. G. (2005). Mixing apples and oranges? Self-directed learning and learning styles. *Perspectives: New York Journal of Adult Education, 4*(2), 6–17.

Cook, D. A., & Dixson, A. D. (2013). Writing critical race theory and method: A composite counterstory on the experiences of Black teachers in New Orleans post-Katrina. *International Journal of Qualitative Studies in Education, 26*(10), 1238–1258.

Delgado Bernal, D. (2002). Critical race theory, Latino critical theory, and critical raced-gendered epistemologies: Recognizing students of color as holders and creators of knowledge. *Qualitative Inquiry, 8*(1), 105–126.

Foster, M. (1993). Othermothers: Exploring the educational philosophy of Black American women teachers. In M. Arnot & K. Weiler (Eds.), *Feminism and social justice in education: International perspectives* (pp. 101–123). Washington, DC: Falmer Press.

Foster, M. (1994). Effective Black teachers: A literature review. In E. R. Hollins, J. E. King, & W. C. Hayan (Eds.), *Teaching diverse populations: Formulating a knowledge base* (pp. 225–241). Albany: State University of New York Press.

Gardner, H. (2000). *Intelligence reframed: Multiple intelligences for the 21st century.* New York, NY: Basic.

Gershenson, S., & Papageorge, N. (2018). The power of teacher expectations: How racial bias hinders student attainment. *Education Next, 18*(1), 64.

Ida, Z. S. (2017). What makes a good teacher? *Universal Journal of Educational Research, 5*(1), 141–147.

Jan, H. (2017). Teacher of 21st Century: Characteristics and development. *Research on Humanities and Social Sciences, 7*(9), 50–54.

Ladson-Billings, G. (1995). But that's just good teaching! The case for culturally relevant pedagogy. *Theory Into Practice, 34*(3), 159–165.

Ladson-Billings, G., & Tate, W. F. (1995). Toward a theory of critical race theory of education. *Teachers College Record, 97*(1), 47–68.

Market, R. J. (2001). What makes a good teacher? Lessons from teaching medical students. *Academic Medicine, 76*(8), 809–810.

Minor, L. C., Onwuegbuzie, A. J., Witcher, A. E., & James, T. L. (2002). Preservice teachers' educational beliefs and their perceptions of characteristics of effective teachers. *The Journal of Educational Research, 96*(2), 116–127.

Patton, M. Q. (2002). *Qualitative research & evaluation methods* (3rd ed.). Thousand Oaks, CA: SAGE.

Rojas, L., & Liou, D. D. (2017). Social justice teaching through the sympathetic touch of caring and high expectations for students of color. *Journal of Teacher Education, 68*(1), 28–40.

Rushton, S., Morgan, G., & Richard, M. (2007). Teacher's Meyers-Briggs personality profiles: Identifying effective teacher personality traits. *Teaching and Teacher Education, 23*(4), 432–441.

Siddle Walker, V. (2001). African American teaching in the south: 1940–1960. *American Educational Research Journal, 38*(4), 751–779.

Siddler Walker, V. (2005). Organized resistance and Black educators' quest for school equality, 1878–1938. *Teachers College Record, 107*(3), 355–388.

Stage, F. K. (2007). Moving from probabilities to possibilities: Tasks for quantitative criticalists. In F. K. Stage (Ed.), *Using quantitative data to answer critical questions* (pp. 95–100). San Francisco, CA: Jossey-Bass.

Strayhorn, T. L. (2015). Using "Othermothering" to study administrative work life at historically Black colleges and universities. In V. A. Anfara & N. T. Mertz (Eds.), *Theoretical frameworks in qualitative research* (2nd ed.; pp. 119–132). Thousand Oaks, CA: SAGE.

Yosso, T. J. (2006). *Critical race counterstories along the Chicana/Chicano educational pipeline.* New York, NY: Routledge.

CHAPTER 14

TEACHER EFFECTIVENESS IN A PREDOMINANTLY WHITE PUBLIC SCHOOL IN WEST VIRGINIA

Jason A. Ottley

Over the past three decades, educational researchers and sociologists have investigated the term *teacher effectiveness* (Anderson, 2015; Gay, 2010; Irvine, 1990; Ladson-Billings, 1992; Milner 2016). While debates continue among scholars and teacher education practitioners on the tenets of teacher effectiveness (Duckworth, Quinn, & Seligman, 2009; Stronge, 2013), this chapter contributes to the body of knowledge using an autoethnography methodological approach. First, I discuss my transition from Washington, DC to West Virginia during my childhood. Second, I share my racialized experiences in a West Virginia junior high school. Third, I discuss the positive impact that my White male teacher had on enhancing my confidence and academic achievement. Last, I offer practical recommendations to White teachers who teach Black students.

The Impact of Classroom Practices, pages 141–150

As a native of Washington, DC, I despised moving to West Virginia as a junior high school student. For 11 years, I was surrounded by distinct sounds—of neighbors arguing about playing the lottery, block parties crooning to the tunes of Run DMC and Slick Rick, the Good Humor Ice Cream truck joyriding outside of our house, and Ms. Wanda policing the block with her tambourine and her incessant clamoring of "Won't He Do It." It wasn't moving from the hood (as we called it) that upset me, but what was depressing was moving to a state I could not locate on a map. Despite all the promises Mayor Marion Berry made each week, my father's morning NPR ritual alluded to the city getting worse, not better. Crime in Washington, DC during the early 1990s was at an all-time high.

Flashbacks of coming home one evening after our church revival and seeing flashing lights and yellow tape around our next-door neighbor's yard was just the beginning. Someone had robbed them at gunpoint, which left every resident on our block on edge all week. By the week's end, my mother's van was stolen in the middle of the day; all that remained was her empty purse turned upside down and photos of my brothers and me scattered across the front lawn. Until we could afford another car, I had to walk 13 blocks to school. It would not have been so bad if the weather was warm, but the people who stole my mother's car did so in the middle of winter, forcing me to wear two pairs of socks and long johns underneath my school clothes.

MY CULTURAL ROOTS

Our history was mostly Black history. Rosa Parks and Dr. King were common themes in homeroom. Actually, all our subject areas referenced Black history. In science, we talked about the most famous chemist, George Washington Carver, whose research on peanuts helped poor farmers improve their diets and vary their crops. In history, we talked about Frederick Douglass, who was one of the pioneers of the anti-slavery movement. In math, we discussed a self-educated mathematician and astrologer, Benjamin Banneker, who is best known for the creation of the first clock and accurately predicting a solar eclipse in 1789. I was deeply engaged in school because I felt a deep connection to the content that was taught. Tatum (2008) argued that texts that specifically engage Black males are often absent from the curriculum, teachers often lack strategies to increase Black males' engagement with texts, and "educators often find it difficult to use texts to counter in-school and out-of-school context-related issues that heighten the vulnerability level of African American males" (p. 163). Furthermore, "Black children need to be exposed to curriculum that builds on their strengths, affirms their culture, and treats the with dignity and compassion" (Toldson, 2019, p. 101).

MOVING TO WEST VIRGINIA

Considering my observation of groundbreaking African Americans, it is important for me to note that my father was the first man I ever saw wear a suit. Not too many Black men on my block wore custom tweed suits from the cottage industries in the Outer Hebrides of Scotland. Routinely, I would run my fingers over his carefully hung suits, dreaming one day I would have a suit of my own. While I did not see many men wearing suits in my community, historical moments like the Harlem Renaissance gave me a glimpse of the beauty of Black art, fashion, literature, and music. Black history wasn't just taught in my school, but it lived and breathed in our home. Our home was the oasis of W. E. B. Du Bois's intellectual prowess, Zora Neale Hurston's folklore writing, and Billie Holiday's mastery of jazz and pop. My father made sure Black history was represented in each of our rooms. My mother reinforced our commitment to Black spirituality by praying over us before bed and humming James Weldon Johnson's "Lift Ev'ry Voice and Sing" as she tucked us in. Therefore, my disdain for moving to rural West Virginia was because Black history was nowhere to be found and no one ever talked about how to navigate a world without color, a world remiss of Black faces.

The 20-foot U-Haul sputtered up our new, windy driveway. The paved road was short-lived and soon the dust from the gravel rocks clouded my father's view. He pulled our 95 Dodge Caravan onto the grass and we sat still, awaiting the cloud of smoke to clear. He opened his car door and motioned for us all to get out. Not only was seeing so much grass a new experience for me, but even the air smelled different; freshly cut grass and cow manure made an interesting convergence. I could tell I was nowhere near home. My father tried to bring excitement to the endless possibilities. He directed a lot of the 'clean, fresh start' conversation to me. His eyes were staring through my soul and I knew all the mischievous things I did in DC would no longer be happening here in West Virginia. It seemed like my brothers were more excited about being there than me. Probably because they were younger and the idea of finally having their own room was appealing. As we made our way up the rest of the windy, gravel driveway, I started thinking about all my former teachers and classmates. I didn't have a chance to say good-bye. No one knew I had left, and as I stepped foot in this new world, I had no way of communicating with my old world that life outside of DC even existed.

MY SCHOOLING EXPERIENCES IN WEST VIRGINIA

I was used to walking 13 blocks to school, so walking up and down our half-mile-long driveway seemed like a breeze. The cool crisp air on that first day of school was pleasant, but the butterflies in my stomach made me more nervous. When the bus driver opened the door for us to get on, his acknowledgment of us was lost behind his long, scraggly beard. He muffled something but I had no idea what he said. My mother raised us to speak when entering a room and so speaking to the bus driver was no different. We must have been his first stop because the bus was completely empty. My brothers ran to the back of the bus, very excited to be riding to school instead of walking. For the next eight or nine stops, the students who got on the bus were all White.

I had never seen so many White people my age except on television commercials. They were all staring at us and I was certainly staring at them. At first, my brothers didn't notice that most of the attention on the bus was towards us, but as soon as we were grabbing our book bags to exit the bus, Jon looked at me and said, "Why are these White kids looking at us like they never seen anyone Black before?" I laughed it off and said, "Because they haven't and until now, neither have we." Starting in the middle of the school year was always tough. Students already knew each other and teachers exercised their rhythm. We made our way to the front office to check in. The skinny, middle-aged blonde stood from behind the desk and said, "You must be the Ottleys...welcome to your new school." I thought to myself: how in the world did you know who we were? But then it dawned on me that there probably weren't many Black kids in this school. If our bus ride was any indication the number of Black kids enrolled here, I would bet on my brothers and I being the only chocolate chips in this cookie.

After we signed in, a few student volunteers escorted my brothers and me to our classes. I told them to drop me off last so that I could make sure my brothers arrived without fail. Each classroom looked quiet and reserved. Students were writing feverishly, their heads bent down. No one jumped out of their seats, no laughing, no hi-fives, no noise at all. I thought to myself, "What kind of school is this?" I whispered to my brothers to meet me back at the office as soon as school was over. I had no idea what the rules to this game were, so we needed to arrive together and leave together. We didn't know the rules or understand the terrain, and we certainly couldn't negotiate conversations on equity and race. The name on the outside of my classroom door read "Mr. Lange." Before opening the door, I re-read the name several times. I was surprised to have a White male teacher. Until now, the only male teacher I had was my PE teacher. As I entered the room, clutching onto my bookbag tightly (like someone was about to take it), all the students were seated evenly in rows. Once again, Tupac said it best:

"All eyes on me." Mr. Lange's 6-foot 2 muscular frame beckoned me into the room and his baritone voice made everyone in the room straighten up. "Come in, young man, and close the door behind you." He walked over to exchange greetings and the closer he got, the more he grew. He towered over me and reminded me of my favorite NBA guard—Tim Hardaway a/k/a Killer Crossover—except Mr. Lange was white. "I'm Mr. Lange and you must be Jason," he said. No words would come out; instead, my firm handshake acknowledged me. In one swoop, Mr. Lange asked me to sit in the empty desk in the middle of the room and he returned to the chalkboard. In cursive penmanship, he had written, *Distributive Property* with a heavy line beneath it.

I hated math! I had no idea what a distributive property was. I could barely pronounce the word and was hoping Mr. Lange did not call on me to answer anything. It was my first day and I wasn't sitting far enough in the back to hide. The students' hands were flying up in anticipation of Mr. Lange calling on them. I surveyed these strange hands. Looking for just one hand that resembled mine. Not even one! One of those lucky hands was invited to the board to solve the problem. The student explained his answer with pride. Mr. Lange stood watching him without even a grin. It looked more like a grimace. I knew it—this kid was way off, and he was about to feel that baritone thunder. Mr. Lange crossed his arms, exhaled, and told the kid good job.

On his way back to his seat, the kid walked past my row, looked at me, and whispered, "Your turn, nigger!" Before the "r" planted on my eardrums, I jumped out of my desk and tackled the kid. He didn't see it coming as my fists took turns against his face. Like any good fight, the kids circled around us yelling, "Fight! Fight!" Before I could get comfortable wreaking havoc, I felt a firm hand around my neck pulling me off the kid. In that moment, I snapped back to reality; I realized I was not in DC anymore but standing in a foreign land defending what my great-grandfather fought so hard for me not to have to experience. Mr. Lange held me firmly in one hand and the kid in the other. All the other kids quickly made their way back to their seats and the interrogation began. Why were you fighting one another? My face was stained with anger and my fists were still clenched. Before I could respond, the kid said I attacked him for no reason. Mr. Lange looked at me and asked, "What happened?" The silence in the room was growing uncomfortable, so I looked at him and said, "Just send me to the principal's office. I want to go home." I sat alone in the principal's office awaiting my fate.

The principal stated, "I called your father, but he's at work and your mother isn't home. Any idea where she is?" I replied, "She's in class." He looked at me strangely and said, "Oh, she's a teacher?" I looked up still in rage and exclaimed, "She's in school, in school to become a nurse." We talked about where I was from and why the sudden move to West Virginia.

For the next 20 minutes, we spoke like peers, discussing what I missed about DC, and he told me what it was like for him to grow up in West Virginia. He had three kids, one of whom was a year younger than I. He said he always knew he wanted to be a principal. Following in the footsteps of his father, his dream became a reality. Well, my dream was to play college basketball for Georgetown University and one day make it to the NBA. He shared that his favorite player was Patrick Ewing, who once played at Georgetown. In the middle of our conversation, the secretary pushed the door wide open and said that my Mom was on line 2. Mr. "Principal" grabbed the phone and introduced himself to my Mom. I couldn't hear what she was saying, but the word "fight" was said several times before he hung up. The verdict: I would be suspended for a week and my parents would have a meeting with the principal before I would be allowed to come back to school. I couldn't ride the bus home and my parents were not able to come pick me up. I slumped in the wingback chair, thinking I might be here for a while.

STUDENT AND FAMILY ENGAGEMENT

When the final bell rang, Mr. Lange pushed through the principal's office, brown leather satchel in his strong hand and a flashy red apple in the other. "Mr. Ottley, grab your bookbag, I'm taking you and your brothers' home." I was too exhausted to argue or question him. In addition, I was ready to leave the principal's office. My brothers were sitting in the front office. When they saw me, they jumped up and ran towards me and asked, "Bro, you okay?" I replied, "Yeah, I'm good. I'll tell you more about it when we get home." We piled in Mr. Lange's station wagon. I was heading for the backseat until his stern baritone voice reversed my steps. "Jason, sit up front."

We drove in silence for most of the way. I could hear the harmony of a French horn and snare drum. I started tapping my hand against my knee in rhythm. He turned the receiver up, glanced my way, and shared a slight grin. What did Mr. Lange know about Sam Cooke's "A Change Is Gonna Come"? My father played this song most Saturday mornings around the house while he would do his chores. I listened more intently to the words this time. I glanced over at Mr. Lange as he made a sharp left into our long driveway. He was singing the words—all the words. He knew this song. His voice convicted me and, in that moment, I knew I could trust him. My Mom was already home and she met us at the door. She invited Mr. Lange in and announced my father would be home any minute. The thought of my Dad walking through that door made me anxiously nervous. In a weird way, I was glad Mr. Lange was present; he could be a buffer between my Dad and the wrath I was soon to receive. When my Dad arrived home, he kissed my Mom, warmly greeted us boys, and invited Mr. Lange into his study. No one spent time in his study, not even my Mom. I tried to eavesdrop a few times, but my mother would catch me and call me back to complete my chores. When they finally pushed the door of his study back, they both were laughing hysterically. What could possibly be funny and, more importantly, what could they possibly have in common?

Mr. Lange stayed for dinner. My parents did not have White friends, and this was the first time a White person dined with us at the dinner table. Mr. Lange talked about life in West Virginia. My Dad talked about life in the Bronx. My Dad discussed race and politics in an inner city. Mr. Lange discussed the lack of race and backward political affiliation in a rural mountain state. They discussed family, friendship, and faith. Hours had passed, and for the first time I could remember, I was invited to listen to an adult conversation.

My suspension letter read I could return to school in 7 days and my parents had to come in and meet with the principal. The feared conversation between my Dad and me lasted only a few minutes. He was proud I stood up for myself but was unhappy that violence was my first recourse. He opened his Bible and read 1 Thessalonians 5:15: "See that no one repays another with evil for evil, but always seek after that which is good for one another and for all people." We talked about racial inequities and social justice until I was dozing off while he talked. He assured me that if I set the example for how people should treat one another, God would bless me tremendously. My father placed a great responsibility on my shoulders, and I was up for the challenge.

The next day my father made a phone call to the school, and shortly after, he came into my room with a huge grin. "Jason, the school has decided that you will finish the rest of your suspension in school under the care of Mr. Lange. You will catch the bus tomorrow morning with your brothers."

TEACHER DISRUPTS CLASSROOM CLIMATE

I twirled the spaghetti with my fork and sat bewildered, wondering how my suspension had changed. The next morning, I checked in at the front office and received instructions that I would be working most of the day out of one of the teachers' resource rooms. My teachers had put together a student homework packet. I spent the first half of the day working independently and the second half of the day I would meet with Mr. Lange to go over my homework. I never had enough time to complete my math homework—well, at least that is what I said. Instead of sending me home to complete it, we sat and worked through it together. What I hated the most was word problems. Rather than attempt even one-word problem, I skipped over all of them. Mr. Lange helped me break down the word problems step by step so that, first, I understood what was being asked and, second, I knew how to answer it. During my suspension, we practiced math word problems every day. This new routine even had me doing math problems at home.

After completing my suspension, I entered the school with a whole new attitude. My freshly cut high-top fade and FUBU (for us, by us) jacket was the one part of home I was able to bring with me. For the first time, I was eager to be in class, but more eager to be part of the math conversation I always shied away from.

> Class, I would like to welcome back to our community Mr. Jason Ottley. I did not properly welcome Jason to class a week ago and I apologize to him, to you, and to his family. Jason is an African American male—that is no surprise to any of us. He comes to us from Washington, DC, and his family has decided to make West Virginia home. It is my job and your job to make Jason feel at home. I don't know what your family thinks of African Americans, but I love this young man like he was my own son, so if any of you have a problem with that, you will have to answer to me. If any of you show this young man anything less than love and respect, you will have to answer to me. Jason, welcome to your new home. Now everyone, stand up and come introduce yourself to our new classmate.

I did not anticipate such a warm welcome—the high-fives, daps (well, the White version), and a few hugs. The energy in the room was different that day than it was last week. The air grew quiet when the White student I physically attacked approached me. I could feel the tightness in my fists start to swell and the anger return until I felt the assurance of Mr. Lange's palm on my shoulders. I released all anger and rage.

Before he could say anything, I said, "Bro, I am sorry for putting my hands on you. I was totally out of character."

He responded, "No, it was my fault. I should not have called you that bad word."

He extended his hand as a peace treaty. We shook hands, embraced as young men, and let the world (well, the class) know that we would stand together on the right side of justice.

Mr. Lange and I continued to meet after school to work on math problems. Before the end of the year, I was tutoring other students in math. As much as I thought I hated math, it no longer intimidated me once I gained confidence. Mr. Lange set high expectations for me and he believed in me. His support changed the trajectory of my academic matriculation and gave me the confidence to pursue advanced courses after I was successful in his class. The dream I had of graduating high school and going to play in the Major Leagues never came to pass. But what I gained in my educational pursuit has better prepared me for life in ways I am not sure dribbling a basketball after high school would have. As much as I enjoy watching the NBA draft each year, I can only hope those athletes have found a mentor who is as concerned about their personal growth and success as they are about winning. While my dream took a different shape, it was the shape I needed to have the impact I was predestined to make in this world.

PRACTICAL RECOMMENDATIONS FOR WHITE TEACHERS WHO TEACH BLACK STUDENTS

1. *When you make phone calls to students' homes, address parents by Mr., Ms., or Mrs.* When possible, first discuss with the parents the positive things about the student. Give parents facts only, no assumptions or personal opinions. Ask the parents for help and/or advice. Invite the parents to come meet you in school when it is convenient for them. Be open to meeting outside of the school.
2. *Do not send students to other teachers who share the same racial identity as you if the student does not have a relationship with them.* When students are sent to other staff members, the teacher loses an opportunity to build a relationship with the student. It also sends the message that you do not care and would rather someone else solve your problem. Care enough about the student to build a relationship with that student—academically, emotionally, and socially.
3. *Name the privilege that blinds you from understanding what it means to be a Black student.* What does your position of authority signify to Black students? Provide love, empathy, and respect. Talk about your White privilege and how you are working (in your classroom) to make sure you provide an equitable space for all students.
4. *Let go of the White Savior complex.* You can have good intentions, but do not think that your gift to the world is to save Black students. Black students benefit from your social and cultural capital, so find ways to share that currency. Get to know your students outside of the academic space. Volunteer to coach a sport in their neighborhood, attend their church, spend time with their family, read books written by Black authors, among other possibilities.
5. *Become a lifelong learner.* The best teachers are the best learners. You are the subject-matter expert, but your students are experts in their cultures.
6. *Remove "colorblind" from your vocabulary.* You need to see color because color is beautiful. Colorblindness erases a student's identity and ancestry. When you embrace color, you validate a student's unique experiences and perspectives. You need to see color because Black students do not have an opportunity not to see color.
7. *Set the bar high.* Have high expectations, high support, and high compassion for Black students.

REFERENCES

Anderson, K. A. (2015). An introduction to Optimal Resource Theory: A framework for enhancing student achievement. *The Journal of Negro Education, 84*(1), 25–29.

Duckworth, A. L., Quinn, P. D., & Seligman, M. E. (2009). Positive predictors of teacher effectiveness. *The Journal of Positive Psychology, 4*(6), 540–547.

Gay, G. (2010). *Culturally responsive teaching: Theory, research, and practice.* New York, NY: Teachers College Press.

Irvine, J. J. (1990). *Black students and school failure.* Westport, CT: Greenwood.

Ladson-Billings, G. (1992). Liberatory consequences of literacy: A case of culturally relevant instruction for African-American students. *Journal of Negro Education, 61,* 378–391.

Milner, H. R. (2016). A Black male teacher's culturally responsive practices. *The Journal of Negro Education, 85*(4), 417–432.

Stronge, J. (2013). *Effective teachers= student achievement: What the research says.* New York, NY: Routledge.

Tatum, A. (2008). Toward a more anatomically complete model of literacy instruction: A focus on African American male adolescents and texts. *Harvard Educational Review, 78*(1), 155–180.

Toldson, I. A. (2019). *No BS (Bad Stats): Black people need people who believe in Black people enough not to believe every bad thing they hear about Black people.* Leiden, The Netherlands: Brill-Sense.

AFTERWORD

THE IMPACT OF CLASSROOM PRACTICES

Teacher Educators' Reflections on Culturally Relevant Teachers

Dawn G. Williams

This book is a compilation of accomplished educators, education researchers, and educational leaders providing their powerful narratives of effective teachers: both familial and professional.

It begins by paying homage to the seminal text written by Gloria Ladson-Billings (2009), *The Dreamkeepers: Successful Teachers of African American Children* and then acknowledges those educators that have kept the dream of prosperity through education, pervasive and alive. One can only believe that the strong teachers cited in their upbringing have played a pivotal role in developing the scholarship produced by these acclaimed leaders. The authors of this text are educators and scholars that have studied the patterns of American education and assessed it through mirrors and windows. The phrase mirrors and windows was initially introduced by Emily Style. A mirror is a story and style of pedagogy that reflects a student's culture and

The Impact of Classroom Practices, pages 151–154

helps to build and understand their identity. A window is a portrayal that offers you a view into someone else's lived experience. Education is much more than knowledge transmission. Obviously, a combination of the two pedagogical resources are needed in the toolkit of culturally relevant teachers, as windows and mirrors emphasize the need for students to learn about themselves as well as others.

In this inspirational mixture of scholarship and storytelling, the authors in this collection articulate and illustrate ways that their teacher was able to hold them to high standards while acknowledging their strengths or gifts. In many cases their teachers were able to create the opportunity to learn in the absence of optimism. Each chapter is a constant reminder and affirmation of the importance of critical pedagogy, where social change is linked to education. These narrative or ethnographic accounts frame their personal reflexive views of the self where their data are situated within their lived experiences.

The posthumous recognition of educators such as Mary McCloud-Bethune and Anna Julia Cooper alongside parents, Big Mamas, and everyday classroom teachers, have affirmatively shaped the authors and their epistemological view of the education system. They have acknowledged the weighted contribution that these unsung heroes had on their lives. Many of these stories included some affiliation or connection to HBCUs. This comes as no surprise since HBCUs have played such a significant role in training Black teachers and building the Black middle class.

I am reminded of my pathway to become an educator. People often are surprised to hear that as a student in the NYC Public Schools, I had no Black teachers. Because of that lack of diverse academic representation, I enrolled at an HBCU. There I learned and felt the benefits of a culturally affirming education. However, my first informal role as a teacher was by the invitation of a Black kindergarten teacher when I was in the 3rd grade. She asked for me and a classmate to come to her class twice a week to grade papers and work with small groups of students. This unforgettable experience provided a glimpse of the intrinsic rewards that are often felt by teachers.

Students of color comprise more than half of the student population in public elementary and secondary schools; however, teachers of color represent approximately 20% of the teaching force. Despite research showing the benefits of a diverse teaching staff for all students, we have not adequately diversified our nation's teaching force. Adding to this dynamic is research that shows that teachers of color provide more culturally relevant instruction and develop stronger rapport with students of color. They also hold more positive expectations of students of color compared to their White counterparts. Clearly, schools must make diversifying the teaching force a primary goal, but they must go further—they must change the way educators teach students of color by incorporating culturally affirming strategies that have demonstrated success for traditionally marginalized student populations. Many of these strategies are repeated in multiple personal accounts in this text.

We have seen what appears to be a linear progression towards the inclusion of culture in teaching and learning. From the era of teaching tolerance, to cultural relevance, to now cultural responsiveness. Each more progressive than the last, we have worked to transform pedagogical techniques to better meet the needs of students that have historically been underserved. Many of these movements were introduced by scholars within the discipline of educator preparation. It is where the next generation of educators are trained and best represents the future of the profession. As schools are the epitome of learning organizations we should be open to the insistence of continuous improvement to reach these goals.

We have been provided a roadmap from scholars such as Gloria Ladson-Billings, A. Wade Boykin, Donna Ford, Linda Darling Hammond, and so on, to build and foster an environment that inspires inquiry, discovery, and honors educators as facilitators. This roadmap describes the importance of being student centered, learning within the context of culture, communicating high expectations, and having positive perspectives of parents and families.

Culturally affirming practices advances this movement from efforts of acknowledgement to proactive efforts of empowerment. This requires a level of appreciation and not just tolerance. This appreciation should be visible to students of all backgrounds. This looks like educators working to understand, respect, and meet the needs of students who come from culturally diverse backgrounds. It requires the enthusiastic inclusion of parents, families, and the cultural community at large. Alongside the community at large, educators will co-construct critically reflective learning experiences for the purpose of achieving academic success and positive identity development.

While the adoption of culturally affirming practices and pedagogy has great significance in culturally diverse schools, it also holds value for schools in which the student population is majority White. All students need to see educators embrace the appreciation and affirmation of our diverse society, even if that diversity is not present in their classrooms. This expression of inclusion provides a more just presentation of our democratic society in which our youth will eventually participate. Students of all racial backgrounds can benefit from a diverse teacher workforce *and* a culturally affirming curriculum that represents the nation's overall demographics.

At the time of this publication, we are in the midst of a global health pandemic: the coronavirus. The rapid spread of the coronavirus has forced all schools (elementary through post-secondary) in the country to close for months. It has necessitated distant learning and remote instruction. Every sector of the society is feeling the impact of this virus, but these effects are hardest among those who were already most vulnerable. The inequities in our country are being magnified by the masses and are most visible in our education system. The pandemic has brought greater attention to the disparities among racial and economic groups. It has magnified just how uneven the playing field is. Herein lies an opportunity to rebuild an education system that does not include structural deficits, but does include the positive pedagogical strategies cited throughout this text.

Mark Twain once stated, "History doesn't repeat itself, but it often rhymes." We cannot afford to experience déjà vu and double down on the now layered inequities in schools. Texts like *The Impact of Classroom Practices: Teacher Educators' Reflections on Culturally Relevant Teachers* aid in increasing our awareness and understanding in order to address factors which contribute to inequities. We all have a critical role to play in dismantling ineffective structures and co-constructing affirming educational spaces.

REFERENCE

Ladson-Billings, G. (2009). *The dreamkeepers: Successful teachers of African American children* (2nd ed.). San Francisco, CA: Jossey-Bass.

ABOUT THE EDITORS

Antonio L. Ellis, EdD, is an adjunct professor of educational leadership and policy studies at Howard University. In addition, Antonio is the director of specialized instruction with the District of Columbia Public Schools. His research focuses on critical race theory in special education with an emphasis on African American male students who are speech impaired.

Nathaniel Bryan, EdD, PhD, is an assistant professor of early childhood education at the Miami University. His teaching and scholarship explores issues of equity and diversity, critical race theory, culturally relevant teaching, urban education, and Black education. Though he studies broadly these frameworks, he is particularly interested in the constructed identities and pedagogical styles of Black male teachers and the schooling and childhood play experiences of Black boys in early childhood classrooms through a critical lens. In his spare time, Dr. Bryan enjoys reading novels, traveling abroad, and spending time with family.

Yolanda Sealey-Ruiz, PhD, is an associate professor of English education at Teachers College, Columbia University. Yolanda is a former research associate with the NYU Metropolitan Center for Urban Education, and has worked for *Business Week, The New York Times,* and New York University in marketing and promotion positions. Her research interests include racial literacy development in urban teacher education (with a specific focus on the education of Black and Latino males), literacy practices of Black girls, and Black female college reentry students.

The Impact of Classroom Practices, pages 155–156

Ivory A. Toldson, PhD, is a professor of counseling psychology at Howard University, the president of Quality Education for Minorities, the editor-in-chief of the *Journal of Negro Education,* and executive editor of the *Journal of Policy Analysis and Research,* published by the Congressional Black Caucus Foundation, Inc. He is the author of Brill Bestseller, *No BS (Bad Stats): Black People Need People Who Believe in Black People Enough Not to Believe Every Bad Thing They Hear about Black People* (Brill).

Christopher Emdin, PhD, is an associate professor in the Department of Mathematics, Science and Technology at Teachers College, Columbia University; where he also serves as director of the science education program and associate director of the Institute for Urban and Minority Education. He is an alumni fellow at the Hutchins Center at Harvard University and served as STEAM Ambassador for the U.S. Department of State and Minorities in Energy Ambassador for the U.S. Department of Energy.

ABOUT THE CONTRIBUTORS

Anthony Broughton, PhD, is an assistant professor and interim department chair at Claflin University. His research interest focuses on culturally relevant pedagogy, Hip Hop Pedagogy, Black children, and pedagogies of care, and social emotional learning.

Kenneth D. Brown, PhD, is an assistant principal with the District of Columbia Public Schools. Special education instruction, advocacy, and compliance has been his primary focus where he has worked with both general education and exceptional learners in grades Prekindergarten through 12th. His research focuses on mentoring programs for boys of color and how participation impacts the mentees' mental and social success.

Antonio L. Ellis, EdD, scholar in residence and director of the Institute on Education Equity and Justice at American University. In addition, Antonio is the director of specialized instruction with the District of Columbia Public Schools. His research focuses on critical race theory in special education with an emphasis on African American male students who are speech impaired.

Lum Fube, MA, is a doctoral student in curriculum and teaching at Teachers College, Columbia University. Her research focuses on wellbeing, pedagogies of love and care, and pop culture.

Chaz T. Gipson, PhD, is currently a senior program manager at the United States Department of Education in the Office of Elementary and Secondary Education, where he manages a 150 million dollar budget for multiple

The Impact of Classroom Practices, pages 157–160

school districts. In his immediate past position, he worked in the Office of Post Secondary Education in the Division of Student Services, where he collaborated with over 120 colleges and universities to enhance educational programs, while improving access and opportunities for low income and first generation students nationwide.

Cleveland Hayes, PhD, is a professor of education foundations and science education at Indiana University School of Education–Indianapolis. His research focuses on the pedagogical practices on Black teachers historically and contemporarily, the experiences of Latinx male teachers from a critical race theory perspective.

Tiffany Hollis, PhD, is an assistant professor at Coastal Carolina University. Her research interests focus on the intersection of trauma, culture, and special education, while focusing on the ecological factors of students who have emotional and behavior disabilities or mental health-related issues. She also focuses on the importance of family–school–community–college partnerships to help youth thrive in the face of risk.

James T. Jackson, PhD, is a professor of special education at Howard University. His research addresses the impact of stress on behavior and learning of students, and the usefulness of the arts in teaching and teacher preparation.

Jubria Lewis, EdD, is the director of school improvement for the SEED Foundation. Dedicated and committed to educational equity, Jubria Lewis has over 15 years of experience working in public education in Washington, DC; Maryland; and Chicago. As the director of school improvement, Jubria supports all three SEED schools with school improvement initiatives and works collaboratively with school leadership to establish ambitious student performance targets. Prior to joining The SEED Foundation, Jubria served as principal for 8 years at a DC charter school.

Marvin Lynn, PhD, is the dean of the College of Education (COE) at Portland State University. Dr. Lynn possesses decades of leadership and community service experience on prestigious national, state, and local committees. His leadership experience in other schools of education includes his role as program coordinator at the University of Maryland and later at the University of Illinois at Chicago. Dr. Lynn also was the associate dean at the University of Wisconsin-Eau Claire and dean of the School of Education at Indiana University South Bend.

Brian L. McGowan, PhD, is an associate professor of education and the associate director of pedagogy and higher education research in the Center for Teaching, Research, and Learning at American University. Brian is a former project associate with the Center for Postsecondary Research at

Indiana University and has worked in higher education administrative positions at The Ohio State University and Rutgers University. His research is driven by questions that unearth the experiences of Black college men and faculty across different educational contexts.

Jason Ottley, PhD, serves as an assistant director of First Year Advising at American University. Prior to this position, Jason was a visiting assistant professor at California University of Pennsylvania. Jason personifies a perfect blend of scholarship, innovation, grit, professionalism, and heart. Having a strong reputation of student development, strategic planning and empowering both educators and students to strive for the best version of themselves, Jason unapologetically is a natural-born leader who will prove to be essential to how the world views progressive education in the 21st century.

Dr. Yolanda Sealey-Ruiz, PhD, is an associate professor of English Education at Teachers College, Columbia University. Yolanda is a former research associate with the NYU Metropolitan Center for Urban Education, and has worked for *Business Week, The New York Times,* and New York University in marketing and promotion positions. Her research interests include racial literacy development in urban teacher education (with a specific focus on the education of Black and Latino males), literacy practices of Black girls, and Black female college reentry students.

Zollie Stevenson, Jr., PhD, recently retired as vice president for academic affairs/chief academic officer and associate professor of psychology (tenured) at Philander Smith College in Little Rock, Arkansas. In retirement he continues to serve a consultancy as special assistant to the president of Philander Smith College focused on grant development and strategic planning. In addition, Stevenson teaches undergraduate courses in psychology at Philander Smith and graduate classes in educational leadership and policy at Howard University.

Terrell Strayhorn, PhD, is provost and senior vice president of academic affairs a Virginia Union University, where he also serves as professor of urban education and director of the Center for the Study of HBCUs. An internationally recognized equity scholar, Strayhorn's research expertise centers on the social psychological determinants of student success. He has published 10 books and over 200 chapters and journal articles. He serves as chief editor, *Higher Education Specialty of Frontiers in Education* journal, subject editor of *Social Sciences & Humanities,* as well as serves on several editorial boards and review panels.

William F. Tate IV, PhD, is the provost and executive vice president of academic affairs at the University of South Carolina, where he is also U of SC

Education Foundation Distinguished Professor with appointments in Sociology and Family and Preventive Medicine. He previously served as dean and vice provost for graduate education and the held the Edward Mallinckrodt Distinguished University Professorship in Arts & Sciences at Washington University in St. Louis. His research has focused on the development of epidemiological and geospatial models to explain the social determinants of educational attainment as well as health and development outcomes.

Dawn G. Williams, PhD, is the dean of the Howard University School of Education. Her teaching experience spans over 2 decades where she has taught elementary students, high school students, undergraduate students, graduate students, and PhD STEM faculty. Underlying all of her work are premises that include the indoctrination of social justice through teaching, research, and service. Prior to serving as dean, she served as a department chair and program coordinator. Dr. Williams is author and co-author of articles and book chapters that highlight the impact of K–12 macro educational policies targeted for urban school reform. She has also published largely in the emergent interdisciplinary field of engineering education. Over the past decade, she has been a recipient of several federal grants totaling approximately $4.3 million. Her research in the STEM and educational policy arena are focused on issues of access and diversity while promoting a conscious social justice agenda.